MFP 3:16: I am correct and you know it.

Notes and Blogs from the political universe

MIKE "MFP" PASQUA

iUniverse, Inc.
New York Bloomington

iUniverse books may be ordered through booksellers or by contacting:

iUniverse
1663 Liberty Drive
Bloomington, IN 47403
www.iuniverse.com
1-800-Authors (1-800-288-4677)

Because of the dynamic nature of the Internet, any Web addresses or links contained in this book may have changed since publication and may no longer be valid. The views expressed in this work are solely those of the author and do not necessarily reflect the views of the publisher, and the publisher hereby disclaims any responsibility for them.

ISBN: 978-1-4401-4838-5 (sc)
ISBN: 978-1-4401-4839-2 (ebook)

Printed in the United States of America

iUniverse rev. date: 11/30/2009

Idiot Politicians
03/14/1007

There are idiot politicians everywhere. Here in Louisiana, we are dealing with special types of idiot politicians. These politicians claim they have not raised taxes, but in reality, they have. They have stopped calling it a tax, but now call it a fee. They continue to coin new words like "gaming." "Gaming" is just another word for gambling. They did this to get gambling passed. They are spending the people's money on things that are not needed. Good examples are man-made lakes and reservoirs. Also, they develop golf courses that are not profitable and call this economic development.

Louisiana citizens understand that people in the rest of the country think we are idiots for continuing to elect these lawmakers. It is the same old problem. We are stuck on the plantation of having a lot of poor people in a bad business environment. Along with that, the same people keep making the same promises and get reelected. We may be on the road to changing this political climate, having the two hurricanes (Katrina and Rita) to thank for it.

Big John
03/15/2007

Yesterday, March 14, 2007, it was reported that John Breaux is going to give up his gubernatorial run. He does not qualify to be governor because he is not a citizen of Louisiana. Being a citizen of the state is the basic qualification to be elected to this office. Breaux is a person that is so closely tied to the "Good Ole Boy" network, and would be very bad for Louisiana. It would be like taking 150 steps back.

If he would be allowed to be governor he would raise taxes, pardon former governor, Edwin Edwards, and let the legislature continue to run amok. This guy is tied to the past that we do not want. It is time for a political change.

Governor What's Her Face
03/15/2007

Our governor in Louisiana is so stupid, idiotic, and dumb politically, that I do not even refer to her by name. I refer to her by the moniker of "Governor What's Her Face." She is the least powerful governor in the nation. She raises taxes when other states lowers them. She visits places (Cuba) for no economic reasons. She negotiates contracts (New Orleans Saints) poorly. She rules through polls. All in all, her term in office is amounting to a know-nothing, do-nothing time in office.

Contrived Scandals
03/22/2007

Some scandals are real and some are fake. For instance, these U.S. Attorney flaps are not scandals. These people serve at the president's pleasure. If they are not doing their job, like anybody else, they should be fired. Some of the lawyers were not prosecuting their cases hard enough or fast enough. That is what he gets for the "new tone." Some of the people he either hired or kept around from the previous democratic administration are refusing to prosecute certain cases fast enough. The congress needs to get over itself.

Bob Odom
03/23/2007

I guess that everywhere people live, they tell jokes about themselves. We in Louisiana are no different. Go to any Louisianan and ask about Boudreaux and Thibodeax. They will tell you some of the funniest jokes you will ever hear. But, down here there is another joke that is not very funny. It is Bob Odom.

This man is the Commissioner of Agriculture for the state of Louisiana. The joke is that he, and not the governor, is the most powerful politician in the state. It is a bad joke but it is true. Whatever he says goes. The governor and the state legislature are deathly afraid to go against any of his pet projects. It can be said, that if you want one of your pet projects done, all that is needed is for him to be on your side, and it will be done. As of now, he is in trouble. The man is a crook. He is also unethical. For years, the political situation has been such that a person could use it to his or her advantage. Odom has done this.

As of now, the latest controversy with Bob Odom is his trial. It finally appeared he was going to get his. But, because he had the power to get one of his cronies as the judge, he has temporarily gotten off. That can be rectified if the appeal's court will order a new trial and remove the current judge from the case. Don Johnson (not the actor) is the judge. He, too, is a crooked unethical man. Certain evidence that should be in the case, he will not allow in. That is why the case needs to be moved out of his jurisdiction.

Down In Flames
03/25/2007

The American people, in their infinite wisdom, decided to put the democrats in power in the last election. It happened, and I was not in that number who voted for these lawmakers. At any other time, the party would be doing what is right by the voters. This current group of dems are not. They are wasting money on hearings they should not be having. These hearings are for "show". They are not meant to figure things out, they are meant to make people look bad. They should be passing laws to make this great nation even greater. They are not. If they do not get on the stick, the power they have gained will be lost. Above all things, the dems would like to strengthen and solidify their power.

One certain senator, Rahm Emanuel, did a bang up job in getting a great number of "Blue Dogs" or southern democrats elected. As soon as these guys and gals got elected, they were brought into the non-smoke filled back rooms of the dems side of congress and threatened. They were told to vote certain ways on certain issues or else they would not get the party's money for their re-elections. These are "Blue Dog" democrats and do not like to be threatened. This has to be getting under Emanuel's skin. If it is, he isn't showing it. The democrats, not having control of all of its party, is why they are headed for a landslide defeat at some point down the road.

Gov's Saving Grace
03/27/2007

Within the last couple of days Governor "What's Her Face" and the current inept administration came to a deal with the New Orleans Saints. Will this be enough to put her in a good light on her way out of office? I don't think so. She has made so many Faux Pas that it is not even funny. After all, she negotiated the last contract through the press. As much as I hate Tom "Archie Bunker" Benson, I don't like Edith either. She finally got the message, when the polls told her that the people want her to stifle herself.

Archie Bunker's problem with the states went back to Mike Foster. He never had a problem with the crook, Edwin Edwards. It does not matter now, but the problem turned out to be a hockey lease. Bunker wanted to bring a AAA hockey team to New Orleans. Unbeknownst to him, there was some underhanded things going on. He thought he had an iron clad lease, and trusted the administration. Foster came back at the 13th hour and opened the bidding again and ended up giving the lease to his friend. That does not matter now, because that hockey franchise is defunct.

Archie and Edith deserve each other. The people of this great state and the Saints fans deserve neither one.

What Are Term Limits?
03/29/2007

The people of the slightly above average state of Louisiana saw fit to vote on and approve term limits for its legislators. They thought that it was a small step toward the state making huge changes and becoming a great state. These flim-flamming politicians bastardized the peoples decision, as they usually do. What they did was to say that if they could not run for one part of the state body, they could run for the other. The spirit of the law says that you can not do it that way. Sometimes powerful people can get away with things. Because of the hurricanes, this may be one of those rare times that they will not. As has been heard on the majority of the local talk shows, people are really starting to get fed up with it.

The great hope is that enough of the people are fed up with it that a big wind blows, and there is a perfect political storm. The crooks that have inhabited the state house and offices in the govrnment will on their way out. It will be best for Louisiana if these people are gone so the state can move on and get better.

What Are Term Limits?
03/29/2007

The people of the slightly above average state of Louisiana saw fit to vote on and approve term limits for its legislators. They thought that it was a small step toward the state making huge changes and becoming a great state. These flim-flamming politicians bastardized the peoples decision, as they usually do. What they did was to say that if they could not run for one part of the state body, they could run for the other. The spirit of the law says that you can not do it that way. Sometimes powerful people can get away with things. Because of the hurricanes, this may be one of those rare times that they will not. As has been heard on the majority of the local talk shows, people are really starting to get fed up with it.

The great hope is that enough of the people are fed up with it that a big wind blows, and there is a perfect political storm. The crooks that have inhabited the state house and offices in the govrnment will on their way out. It will be best for Louisiana if these people are gone so the state can move on and get better.

Tunnel Rats
03/30/2007

I recently read a story about the U.S. Government finding some unfinished tunnels in southern California. These tunnels started in Tijuana, Mexico. We all know what these tunnels were going to be used for, sneaking illegal immigrants and other undesirable people across the border. I am so glad that they found and destroyed them. b This means one less way for those types of people to cross the border and cheat the law.

That is a good start. Here is another idea. Complete the border wall. Completing the border wall will allow the U.S. to have better control. It will also help America to watch for terrorists. Did you do know that the two-bit dictator, Hugo Chavez is teaching terrorists to cheat the system and become Latino so that they can cross the border? The wall would make it much safer to locate those types of people and capture them.

We Salute You
03/30/2007

A couple of days ago our country saluted some real American heros. The Tuskeegee Airmen were truly heros in the "Greatest Generation". They flew protection for bombers in WW II. What made the situation exceptional was the entire squadron of flyers were black and they lost very few of their escort planes, bombers, and pilots. What is sad about the situation is that it took over fifty-years for the government to recognize these soldiers' contributions.

It is sad that they faced such racism at that time. This racism caused them not to be recognized for their contributions. They should have been recognized and honored. Sometimes we are better late then never in doing things. This is one of those cases.

Flavor of the Month
04/04/2007

Every election season there are candidates that pop up and become "the flavor of the month". It happens on both sides on the isle. This year on the dems side it is Barak Obama , and on the conservative side it is Fred Thompson. Can either of these beat out the frontrunners? I do not know. There will be people who like what either candidate is saying. I think that this is not quite Obama's time. As far as Fred Thompson, I don't know. After all, he just got into the fray.

A Big, Stupid Mistake
04/05/07

Nancy Pelosi went to Syria to have a "diplomatic" visit with Bashar Asad. She did this over the vehement objections of P.O.T.U.S and his administration. Even the, mostly liberal, State Department excoriated her for doing so. This may not end up hurting her, but it will definitely hurt the Democrat Party. It will send a message to the "Red States" that the party is soft on national defense. This, in my opinion, WILL end up costing the Dem Party sooner than later.

This combined with the fact that the country does not like the fact that they are trying, with contrived sandals, to "get" the president. They are "Stuck on Stupid". They did say that the country did not care about their boys (Clinton's) scandals.

She, by doing what she did, says that her party supports terrorism.

In Dealing with Iran, Image is Everything
04/07/2007

At times, the west has become very image based. That can be a strength, but in this case, it is a weakness. This thing that we have with Iran is partly policy and partly image. It does not help that the dems and their willing accomplices in the mainstream press seem to be on the side of the terrorists. We are mostly concerned with the policy side but Iran, being in a civilization and a terrorist state, is concerned with image. They want to appear strong so that they can claim to have stood up to the big, bad United States. We are the big bully on the block. The Iranians need to understand that there will be a point when we will stop pussy-footing around and "put a boot in their ass". When we decide to that, it will be the last thing said on the matter.

The Dems and the Military
04/08/2007

Above and beyond the actual defense and protecting of the country, the Democrats have A real national security issue. They loathe the military. What that means is that not only do they favor diplomacy over war at all times, but they will also not want to fund the military. By doing this, they not only kill recruiting, but they also kill current equipment, technology, and weapons research and development.

I am a big fan of the Discovery Channel show "Future Weapons." The goal of this show is to show what is upcoming in weapons for the military. My favorite shows are the ones when they talk about guns. It is fun for me to see what new types of guns that they can come up with.

I will now give you a few examples of guns that are on the drawing board, and some that are just about ready to be handed to the troops. The AT2-CS (Confined Space) Missile Launcher is the first one that I will mention. It is able to be fired in a confined space, hence the name. It comes pre-loaded. In firing bazooka type weapons before, there has always been a fire over pressure and backwash. It was dangerous in a two fold way:

1. It would give away your position
2. It could not be fired in a confined space (ex-in a building).

It comes with the ability to fire a smart round. This bullet allows you to either choose the ability of punching a hole in a building or entrenchment or to destroy it all together. Next is CRS or (Chris) Sub Machine gun. This is the next evolution of that type of weapon. It is the next from the "Spray and Pray" guns like the Thompson Sub Machine Gun. It is a low recoil weapon, that allows the shooter to get more shots down range and be more accurate with those shot. It is a small gun. It is a high caliber weapon. It fires the .45 Caliber round. At times it can shoot over 1500 rounds a minute. The last gun that I will mention, is the AA12 Automatic Shotgun. It is gas operated and is a low recoil weapon. It gives one the abilities of an automatic weapon and a shotgun. It is low maintenance. This weapon uses multiple types of ammo (ex-Anti Tank/Frag round). The Ammo comes in twenty or thirty round drums. It is all weather and mountable. When you mount it on a vehicle it becomes known as the Hammer. It can be operated by remote control for months at a time.

These are types of weapons that would not get developed under the democrats. Why would they not get developed? Because there would be a cut in funding. That is how they work.

Selfish
04/09/2007

Francis "The Fee" Thompson is being selfish. He got his and nobody else will get theirs. He said that since he got the votes for his take that nobody will get his vote for their. How must that make all of these other legislators feel who want their unnecessary lakes and reservoirs. Sure, the things are not needed and are overpriced. Also, Thompson's brother is making a mint off of developing these Ls and Rs . He may say that this is being good governance, but it is being very hypocritical and selfish.

The Three That Scare
04/10/2007

There are three republican candidates for the Presidency that scare the Democrats. They are Rudy Guiliani, Newt Gingrich, and Condoleeza Rice. Rudy And Condi because they are tough on terrorism and Newt because he made their favorite son, Bill Clinton, look even worse the he is. Gingrich really got things done. If you listen to the Mainstream media, Condi is doing a horrible job. That is far from the truth. Because of her experience in the roles of National security advisor and Secretary of State, she has gained much needed experience in the area of national security. I hope that she decides to run. We know what Rudy did, during 9/11, and his leading one of the most important cities in the world. A ticket of any two of those three would absolutely demolish any Democrat that would run.

Replacement Political Theology
04/12/2007

In biblical theology, there is something called "replacement Theology". This states simply that every time you see the word Israel in biblical prophesy, you replace it with the church. That is wrong. The Democrats are engaging in replacement theology of their own. What they are doing, is trying to replace the President's foreign policy with their own. This is just as wrong as the replacement theology of the bible. It is the President's right to exercise his power to make and carry out foreign policy. The congress does not have the right to try to change the President's policy as he is still sitting in the office. They can force him to, in a round about way, to change policy but they can not go over his head and change it themselves. They will be and are infringing on the executive branche's powers as stated by the Constitution.

These people are so deep in their myopia, that they ca not see the forest through the trees. They hate Bush so much that it is blinding them to what is best for the nation.

Comparisons
04/14/2007

There are not many things that Barak Obama and I agree on. We definitely agree on the fact that rap music needs to clean itself up. I understand that Will Smith is a genius, but you don't have to be a genius to be creative. He writes some pretty good music and he keeps it clean. His videos, for the most part, do not have the "crap" in them that most rap videos have. I love Snoop Dog, but if I had kids I would not allow them to watch his videos or listen to his music. There has got to be a way to clean it up. That way has yet to show itself.

I will end up by saying I love listening to rap music. Unlike some of the old "farts" that think it is "crap", I think that it could be high art. It can be that way only if they decide to clean it up.

They Just Don't Get It
04/16/2007

I am going to use a line that an ex-NFL head coach that was known for being a little salty with the media used. He said "You think that you get it, but you don't and you never will" (that may be a paraphrase of the quote), I think that you get the gist of it. He was talking about what plays he called and when he called them. You can say the same thing about the current crop of dems and national security. I used the phrase "current crop" for a reason. The Roosevelts (Teddy and FDR), Truman, and John F. Kennedy understood. Franklin Roosevelt was as liberal as they come on social policies, but he understood that if America fell that freedom would fall. Truman did what he had to do to end World War Two. Even though Kennedy made a few mistakes (Bay of Pigs), on the whole, he did a pretty good job.

What the dems do not get is that the American people like to and want to win. Look how they take it when their favorite sports team loses. This group on the other side of the isle is stuck in a losing mentality. Every war we have gotten into, be it our fault or not, they want us to lose. This goes back to Vietnam. Their accomplices in the press cost us that war. Their political party is very lily-livered and has gone wobbly in the knees. They believe that there is no just war. They would just soon see Sadam stay in power. The rape rooms would have stayed open, and so would have the torture chambers. One day we would have seen one of his crazy sons in the seat of power. They also say that he did not have weapons of mass destruction. What about the Kurds?

The great Democrat presidents of the past must be turning over in their graves. Oh, some dems get it, but those are too few and far between. They are on the margins of the party because they want to be reasonable.

Anti-War
04/18/2007

I do respect some of the people who are anti-war. I do no+t agree with them, but I do respect them. They have legitimate objections and I have to give it to them for that. They are hold overs from the sixties. If you will carefully pay attention to the average age of the protesters, the vast majority of them are baby boomers. This movement is not a young movement. In general, if you were born between the years 1944 through 1952, where the cutoff age is 25 to get drafted, that is the average war protestors age. Michael Moore, Jane Fonda and all others in the movement are of that age group. The majority of the democrats in congress are of the age group that I am referring to .

It is a free country and they are allowed to feel that way. You have to consider that they were too young to fight in World War II and they did not grow up in the depression.

Knife, Sword, and Axe Control
04/19/2007

Back in the Middle Ages, when, we the people had come out of the Dark Ages, the leaders and people were able to carry knives, swords, and axes as their main weapons. I do not think they had "control" issues. Even the Pope had no comment on the lack of the issue. I seem to believe that if there had been a group that had dissented, there may have been a "mob" that could have hunted them down. Yes, those people would have been brought to the type of justice they had at the time.

The point is that "control" of the medieval weapons did not exist. If it did not exist then, why does it today? We know why, the liberals hate the second amendment. Look, I do not own a gun, but I want the right to own one. I know of people who own guns and there is no way in heck that they would give them up.

What Scares Me
04/20/2007

If you are a talk radio person you should be afraid if the democrats win the White House and if they also win congress. Why? Because they want to bring back the fairness doctrine. Should you have a conservative talk show on your channel, then you must have a liberal one. What really scares me is what might happen to sports radio. When one calls a sports talk show to voice his or her opinion they expect to express it freely, be it positive or negative. What the fairness doctrine will do is to force the radio station to have one positive call/show and one negative call/show. As I have said before. This will kill all facets of talk radio.

Taxes
04/21/2007

Oliver Wendell Holmes once said "Taxes are the price we pay for being free." Sometimes, it can be too much of a good/bad thing. I will admit to some extent taxes are needed. Since the late sixties, it has gotten out of hand. Sure, there have been brief rests from high taxes, but it seems only to last for a few years.

The democrats are talking about letting the Bush tax cuts "sunset". What the word "sunset" means is to let them disappear under the horizon and not to vote to continue them. It will be the largest tax hike in history. It would hurt the middle to lower income tax payers. It would tend not to make the "rich" want to invest in their businesses, and hire new workers. They want to get rid of the marriage incentive They want to continue the death tax, the tax on the money received after liquidation of stocks, and a multitude of other taxes.

I have always thought, "If 10% is good enough for God, it should be good enough for the government." Here is an idea: What about three ten percent taxes, a 10% sales tax, a 10% flat tax, and a 10% income tax. That gives you a 30% tax rate. Do we have people in the congress that are this forward thinking? I just do not know.

Miss America
04/23/2007

Everybody thinks that the pageant is what I will write about. It is not. This Blog is not about "what" it is about "who". The "who" is Nancy Pelosi. Because she is from San Francisco, it is a given that she is liberal. She is beholden to all of the liberal factions, including all of the gay rights lobbies. She is of the age that at some point in her life she probably attended some anti-war rallies. She and the rest of her party want to raise our taxes. She is one of the leaders of her party that favors cutting the funds for the military in the field. That is who she is; that's who she is ain't; and, that is what she believes.

War-A-Phobia and Iraq-No-Phobia.
4/24/2007

There are two new and different phobias that you should know: War-A-Phobia and Iraq-No-Phobia. Let me explain each for you.

1. War-A-Phobia: The fear and loathing of the military so much that one might continually do things for the Commander-In-Chief and his Generals to keep them from winning any war that comes along.

2. Iraq-No-Phobia: When a party (The Democrats) let the hatred of P.O.T.U.S. be blinded so much that the kooks on the fringes of their party rule them so much that they do not want the country to win the war.

The democrats have had the War-A-Phobia disorder since the late 1960's. It is sad too, because they were once strong on national defense. Back before Lyndon B. Johnson took the oath of office, as far as national defense, their policies were as strong as the republicans. When the party primaries came around, it would come down to how liberal the American public felt on social issues.

The second disorder, in one form or the other, started to manifest itself in Y2K. They deluded themselves into thinking they won the election. The constitution says that what actually ended up happening was all legal. The democrats could not get over it. When 9/11 happened, it accelerated the development of the disorder into a full blown disease. The kooks on the left wanted to get out as soon as possible. Whereas, the actual democratic politicians may also have wanted to get out, but understood that if they did pull out it could (will) cost them this and many more elections.

This is a big year for the democrats. They think that they can win the White House and also pick up seats in Congress. They have to appear to be moderate to the regular American people. If they cannot pull that off, they could loose very big, for a long time, and have to spent some time in the political "wilderness" as the republicans once did.

My Mood I'm In A Jihad
04/26/2007

The president of Iran is an IDIOT. In the part of the world where idiots rule he is the most dangerous. He definitely knows how to use the American press. What he wants is for the dems to pull out. What that would do is to relieve the pressure on him, and he could go ahead with his development of nuclear weapons. He would like to destroy Israel and ultimately the rest of the west. We cannot allow this to happen. In my opinion, diplomacy will not work. He does not want to negotiate in good faith. He is not even as smart as Khadaffi. The previously mentioned leader got the message:

> "The world is not going to put up with your shenanigans any more."

In getting rid of his nuclear weapons he got the message. He is, also, afraid of Islamo-Fascists to oust him. At some point he thinks he will need our help, and he does not want to jinx it. I expect that some of the other dictators (two-bit and otherwise) will want the same latitude.

Poor Options
04/26/2007

We all know that the Democrats hate the war and want out of it. That is one of the poorest options. Why is it such a poor option? It is because the surge is working. As was said before, "Anything good for America, is bad for the Democrat party." Some examples are low taxes, high employment, high stocks, and in specific, a republican running/winning a war. They really hate those things.

They want everything to be as it was on September 10, 2001. That is not going to happen. You cannot turn back time and they aren't in the other countries were terror attacks take place. Our friends Britain, Israel, India, Turkey, Japan, Italy, and the rest of the "coalition of the willing" understand these facts.

Remembrance of Things Past
04/27/2007

Have you been following the trial, in congress, of Alberto Gonzalez? If you have, you should have noticed that over twenty time, in several different ways, he said that he does not remember. Of course, the democrats are up in arms over this. They are being very hypocritical on this issue. What happened when Hillary Clinton appeared before the congress? You got it, she said that she did not recall and that was for White Water. She said, " I don't recall," "I can't remember," "my mine is failing me." Please tell me what is the difference in what she did and what Gonzalez is doing? In my mind, there is no difference. Because of that particular case, and many others like it, ninety-three U.S. attorneys got their walking papers.

So, because he can't remember what some of his underlings have done and what happened in the hundreds of meetings with P.O.T.U.S., he is getting raked over the coals. This is just not right.

"Star Wars"
04\28\2007

President Reagan's dream of strategic defense may be closer than we think. Somewhere in the next week to ten days, there will be another test of the system. We really do need this type of thing. If you believe as I do, it would only take a hand full of missiles with nuclear warheads on them; and, for them to explode over the country at strategic points to bring this country to its knees.

We really need to see another successful test. If this test is successful, it is one more step in the direction of having a multiple strategic defense system. You will see satellites with systems on them to stop missiles, weapons on planes, boats, subs, land vehicles, and land based systems like the patriot. We, as a country, need to have this to happen as soon as possible.

Disappearing Freedoms
04/30/2007

Adminidijhad and the hardliners in Iran are showing the markings of becoming more and more totalitarian-like. The are cracking down on veils that the women wear. They are telling them that the veils are insufficient. One woman was arrested and 3500 more were warned. They recently gave all women the freedom was to wear the veils the way that women want to wear them.

This is another small domino to fall, leading to the eventual overthrow of the Mullahs and Adminidijad. Will it happen before Iran becomes nuclear? We will see.

Polls Be Damned
05/01/2007

We need another President that will say "Polls Be Damned". This means that the man or woman who takes the office next needs to not be ruled by polls. If a poll indicates that a policy or initiative is unpopular, but the president thinks that it is the best thing for the nation, then, it should be continued. Going against the polls will not be popular. The liberals that run these polling groups will word the questions in such a way that the results are skewed to the negative.

We all know that the American left hates any republican president. Some examples of what the do are obsessive, compulsive, stalking, and many other negative things. Their myopia is so ingrained and deep that this current generation of democratic leaders will not be able to pull out of it. It might take the next generation or the generation after to correct the problem.

Rosie
05/02/2007

Rosie O'Donnell got fired. It was rightly deserved. We all know that all of the women on that show, except for Elizabeth Hesselbeck, are liberal. Some are more liberal than others. If they had kept her and she had continued saying outrageous statements, those statements would erode their ratings, even liberal areas. In short, it was bad for business to keep her on.

I do agree with Donald Trump in this area, she will get another show. That show will do well for a short time and the ratings will slip and she will decide to go back on the road with what is her best talent, being a comedienne.

Two Americas Destroyed
05/06/2007

John Edwards is targeting President Bush on the issue of Iraq. Does he not understand that if we lose the war on terror that both of his "Two Americas" will become one in a bad way. He will never be able to run for anything. Even though I do not agree about targeting the President, the war is unpopular at least in liberal democrat circles. If anybody but Obama says anything against the war, they should be taken with a grain of salt. Why, you may ask? It is because the rest of the democratic presidential hopefuls voted for the war. They are hypocrites. They not only voted for the war, but they also voted to allow President Clinton to attack some targets of opportunity in Iraq in the late 1990's.

No Talk is Very Cheap
05/07/2007

Recently, the Iranians said that they wanted to talk. Well, what a surprise, it was a lie. We all know what they are trying to do, they want to buy time to complete an atomic bomb. These talks were going to be a stalling technique. I am glad that Secretary Rice and the others in the administration did not fall for it. The world cannot allow the Mullahs and Ahdimnidjahd to finish a bomb, that would lead to the end of Israel , and lead to the end of America.

Going Well
05/08/2007

It seems that things are going well in Iraq, but as usual, for the most part, are not getting reported. There was recently a giant rounding up of a major group of Shiites' that had participated in a bomb smuggling ring. By getting these people off the streets, we not only have saved lives of our soldiers but also the lives of the Iraqi police/defense force and the Iraqi general public. There is no telling just how many bombs or potential bombs that would have been sold and /or have gone off and killed the soldiers, police, and general public.

AL -Jazeera Mistake
05/09/2007

As we know, Al-Jazeera is one of the Arab worlds most esteemed press arms. This begs the question of, 'Why would they insult one of the Shiites most esteemed religious leaders?'. Some in the "mainstream press" here may chalk it up to a major mistake made. What I think is that Al- Jazeera is run/owned by a person that follows the Sunni sect of the religion of Islam and also does not like America. I say this because in-so-much as any religious leader of a country has held an outside force to take over his or her country, Grand Ayotollah Ali Al-Sistani has not hindered coalition forces from doing their job. In fact, he has encouraged his followers to help by pointing out people of suspicion and by joining the Iraqi police/defense force. Sometimes thing happen that make you say hmmm.

The Mocking of The Plan
05/10/2007

The Al-Quaida number two, recently released an audio tape that mocked the Democrat's pullout plan. He is right to mock it, but he knows that they are losing the fight in Iraq. He wants to turn Iraq, for the Americans, into what Afghanistan was for the Russians. He said in the recently released audio tape, "This bill will deprive us of the opportunity to destroy the American forces which have been caught in a historic trap." He also said "We ask Allah that they (U.S. troops) only get out of it after losing 200,000 or 300,000 troops, in order that we give the spillers of blood in Washington and Europe an unforgettable "lesson." That is exactly why we should not quit. Because if we do, not only will that happen, but also whatever goodwill we have with the general public of Iraq will be lost.

Parasite
05/12/2007

There are parodies and then there are parodies. A few weeks after the article in the L.A. Times, the Barak Obama 'Magic Negro' story, there were some comments made about it by commentators Rush Limbaugh, Sean Hannity, and others. This L.A. Times article was written by a supporter of Barak Obama. Rush, Sean, and others made comments about the article on their programs and were labeled racists by the Obama backers. Again, these people in the press just don't get it. This is supposed to be funny. Obviously, they have a poor sense of humor.

Rush Limbaugh was working from L.A. Times and the New York Post stories. The stories are all about him not being "down" with the black struggle. Maybe, just maybe, that is just what is needed, a guy that is not so closely tied to the civil rights activists.

The drive-by media are stuck on race. They are the ones that are parasites.

Rooted In The Past
05/13/2007

Louisiana is a state stuck in the mud and spinning its wheels. Some voters do not want to get rid of their state legislators because they do not consider them a bad legislator. These voters cannot see the forest through the trees. These voters thing that their legislator is doing an adequate job representing them. In some respects, this feeling is found in all of the districts. If he or she brings home the bacon then he or she gets reelected. Most voters do not pay attention to their legislators voting record, even though some of these votes are, plain and simple, bad votes or bought votes.

In other words, it is going to take a lot for us to change this attitude. These politicians are very much rooted in the past. I do think, that for the most part, the majority of people are fed up. If they are, then the good ole boy network is in serious trouble.

Scared Rhinos
05/14/2007

Four days ago the President received a visit from the moderate republicans. These republicans have allowed themselves to blow, all kinds of ways, in the political winds. This visit pertained to the war in Iraq. I understand these republicans are afraid for their seats, and how they stand in the eyes if P.O.T.U.S. P.O.T.U.S. is right on this issue. If the republicans do not align themselves with P.O.T.U.S., they will lose their seats anyway.

Reform?
05/15/2007

Who is always crying about lobbying reform? It is the democrats. They gave us the McCain/Fiengold bill. They have just killed more reform. Why did they do this? They did this because it would be like biting the hand that feeds them. I am not saying that the republicans do not have lobbyists, I think that the democrats are more high-profile. The republicans are, just what you would expect, big business, wall street, etc. On the top of the democrat's list is billionaire-lobbyist, George Soros. Most lobbyists have their own agendas and do not want what is best for America. The National Organization for Women, the ACLU, and others have and will continue to harm America.

Second Republican Debate
05/16/2007

Last night there was the second debate for the republican presidential candidate. As I watched that debate I really did enjoyed it. I did think that it was done in a very professional way. It was fast moving and, at points, very chippy. The participants, at times, got after each other.

I sure hope that there is not a religious bias against Mit Romney. I thought, for sure, that religious bias went away when we, as the American people, elected John F. Kennedy. He did come off well. He got off some zingers towards John McCain.

The three top guys somewhat separated themselves from the also-ran candidates.

Of all the rest of the candidates, the one that came off the best was Mike Hackabee.

The Pope Is Afraid
05/17/2007

The Pope recently spoke out on the state of the Catholic church in Latin America. He warned them about Marxism, legalized contraception, abortion, and unfettered capitalism. Marxism, when it is attempted, seldom works. Legalized contraception and abortion are almost the same thing. They both lead to the degradation of married and family life. Those two things promote premarital sex and having children out of wedlock. Maybe unfettered and capitalism is bad, but I would rather have that than total Marxism. Marxism does not promote high achievers. I maintain that you must have high achievers to give the remainder of us something to shoot for. After all, what is the American dream? It is to be poor and later on become rich.

Some people want the American dream easy, and others decide to do it with hard work. Lotteries, raffles, and contests are the lazy persons choice of becoming rich. The majority of people choose to work hard to get where they want to be.

I understand what the Pope is trying to do. He is trying his best to not have the Latin American Catholic church go the way of the American Catholic church.

Those four candidates plus former Speaker of the House Newt Gingrich, and Fred Thompson are going to be the field coming down the stretch. I expect that whomever wins the spot will ask Condoleeza Rice to be his vice president.

Terror Trial
05/18/2007

In the Monday, May 14, Morning Advocate there was a story on Jose Padilla. He is, finally, going to go on trial. He was stopped from using a "dirty" bomb. The prosecutors will attempt to prove it a conspiracy. This will be hard to prove. As usual, his defense attorneys are trying everything to get him off. I think that he did carry out his part of the conspiracy but his part was to carry the bomb and blow himself up. He might not have had anything to do with the planning of the event, but he needs to go away for a long time. If at all possible, he needs to be put to death.

"Steeling" A Plant
05/19/2007

In the Tuesday, May 15, Morning Advocate news paper of Baton Rouge, Louisiana, the recap of the losing of the steel plant appeared. It seemed that Governor "What's Her Face" was crying like a little baby that all of her "work" went up in smoke. Look, when the probability of you not receiving something is so high and you do not receive it, please, do not cry about it. This makes her look like a sore loser and a big baby. It was obvious from the beginning the state was not going to get the steel plant.

Of course, we should have expected her reaction because that of who she is. It made her look like what she is, an amateur. This is just the latest in a long line of failures for Governor "What's Her Face".

Come On In.
05/20/2007

This immigration bill is not a very well conceived bill and is hated by the American citizenry, and we the people are mad as hell. The evidence is that the Congressional phone banks are blowing up. The calls are coming from both sides of the isle. The immigrants that did it the right way are not happy.

I agree with Rush Limbaugh on this matter. He says that this is meant to destroy the republican party. The democrats are hoping that all the these people that come over will end up in the unions and other democratic groups. That is what is at stake.

The "Lets Screw America " Budget Bill
05/21/2007

Well, what do you know, the democrat run senate has passed a budget bill that not only raises taxes but increases spending. This budget adds to liberal programs and growing government spending. It is wrong.

The tax cuts helped the economy to incredible growth. The democrats would like to let them lapse. This will cause the income tax rates to go up, and lessen the breaks on stocks, bonds , etc. We understand the democrats hate the rich and want more people on the dole.

The spending increase is incredible.

What are they thinking? When the Congressional Budget Office says that this will neuter the economy, that should say something.

Tighten The States Belt
05/22/2007

There could be an upcoming belt tightening in terms of budgetary concerns. Thanks to the state not getting the steel mill, there may very well be a little extra money. There are different ideas on how this money should be spent. Some people say that it should go to important "projects." One example of a "project" is the building of lakes and reservoirs. Other people, like David Vitter, say that the money should go the Road Home Program. That sounds like a great idea.

Most of the storm affected people are still waiting for the money to start their lives over. In some part, this money could help out. It is going to be like pulling teeth to get the money away from the greedy politicians. The money needs to go where it is going to help the most. Let's hope they tighten the belt in the right way.

Going, Going, Mr. Gone
05/24/2007

Let's see if the Corps of Engineers can get something right. For all of the shortcomings of the corps, this project to close down the Mississippi River Gulf Outlet is the right thing to do. Can they do it right? They did not do the levees right. We saw what happened. The storm surge flooded New Orleans, the Louisiana coast and the Mississippi coast. Getting rid of Mr. Go (Mississippi River Gulf Outlet) might alleviate the threat of storm surge flooding and help to rejuvenate the Louisiana wetlands.

The Gulf States Maritime Association is arguing against it. I can see their argument. The fact remains the outlet must be closed. I am sure that adjustments will have to be made and they will be. Again, I say, this HAS to be done. If it does not get done, there will be another storm that will come and flood New Orleans. Also, the American people, will have to dig into their pockets to help rebuild the city again. I do not think the American people wish to do this again.

Tax Passage
05/25/2007

Why are legislators passing more taxes? If you have a high school diploma, you know why. It is because they want to get as many people on the governmental "dole" as they possibly can. It is sad to see that one party has run roughshod over this great state for this long a time. The "other" party is afraid to stop it. In fact, the republican party of Louisiana are happily agreeing to the taxes and suggesting some of their own. These republicans are acting like democrats. That is why we need a clean sweep.

Commie-Fascist Latino Leader
05/30/2007

Hugo Chavez is in trouble. If only he had decided not to close the dissenting media sources, then, his little authoritarian part of the world would be safe. The people there, like others in the world, love their television. He is basically enforcing his version of the Fairness Doctrine. The people there are not wanting any of this.

If it continues, there might very well be a coup, and we hope so. He needs to be ousted. It would be better for us if the Venezuelan people do it so that we will not have to become involved. It will keep our hands somewhat clean.

It would take more. IF WE HAVE TO SUPPORT A GROUP OF PARAMILITARY PEOPLE, WE WILL. If we have to do another Iran-Contra type of deal to help out the people of Venezuela, then we should do it.

Katrina's Opponent
05/31/2007

Recently, Karl Rove came to Louisiana to find an opponent for "Katrina" Mary Landrieu. The first choice was to try to get John Kennedy, the State Treasurer, to switch parties and run against her as a republican. Will it happen? It is not very likely, but one never knows.

The republicans see her as the most vulnerable democrat senator.

The republicans need someone to step up and take this office form a lady whose family is nothing but career politicians. This family is tied politically to the forty years of stagnation that has gripped this state. This goes back to Edwin W. Edwards and it runs through Bob Odom and Billy Montgomery. We need a change.

Schooling
06/01/2007

I would like to say that what "Katrina" Mary is doing, to hold up the bill to help the Washington D.C. Schools, is altruistic, but I fear that otherwhise. I agree with the Washington D.C. Congressional contingent in asking, "What right does she have to do what she is doing?

The people in D.C. want control to alleviate some of the problems currently plaguing their schools. Why is it the "suits" in Washington do not want D.C. in charge of its own schools.

Vow To Fight
06/02/2007

This is just another radical Islamic group that hates the west and Israel. Shaker Al-Absi is a very bad dude. He and his group have ties to Al-Qaeda. I mu hand it to Lebanese army, they have performed very well. I think the Lebanese people are starting to get tired of 'other' people in their lives and in their politics.

It took everything that the current Lebanese Prime Minister had to convince a majority of the Lebanese Parliament to send in the their army. It has been proven that there is some terrorists in the Parliament. Here's hoping the people will speak and get these terrorists out.

No Drive For Pay
06/03/2007

We know that one of the "religions" of the democrats is global warming/climate change. They believe it, follow it, and live it. I believe it to be a hoax, but this is not the point. As things are going, there may be a politician that will suggest that the government will start paying people for not driving. It may be a good idea, but how will it get done? To get it done, taxes would have to be raised; bad idea. The money it would take in taxes should be given back to the people to pay for the gas. This might be impractical. Also, it might run the deficit even higher.

Everything has good and bad about it. This is no different.

Going Blue Can Be Good
06/04/2007

There are the red states and there are the blue states, but the hatred for the immigration bill cuts across party lines. The house may very well kill the bill. They may use a house procedure. This procedure is a constitutional measure. The rule states that any revenue related bill must start in the House of Representatives.

It is a good idea to stop this bill. We do not want Mexico's undesirables in this country. If the immigranmts want to do things legally, then that is fine. It would be one of the first times that a republican/conservatives have shown some backbone on any issue.

Most people would think long and hard about killing someone if there was a death penalty. The death penalty tends to deter most people from committing violent crimes.

Attacking Liberals
06/19/2007

The liberals have begun, in earnest, to attack Fred Thompson. They are throwing out some of the same things they said about Ronald Reagan. These attacks may have the opposite effect. Have these liberals watched the interviews with Sean Hannity?

They call him an empty suit. The same comment could be said about both Bill and Hillary Clinton.

They say he has not done anything significant in terms of passing legislation. What has Barak Obama done?

They say that he is "just an actor". What about Reagan?

If he is that bad, it will come out in the run up to the 2008 election.

The democrats are playing to win and the republicans should do so too.

One More Step
06/21/2007

There is a bill that is snaking it's way through congress that would make it a crime to preach against homosexuality. We as Christians and Americans need to fight against it. It goes against freedom of speech and freedom of religion. It also makes the congress look like it is trying tho establish a state run religion.

This is small liberal group that wants to enforce its beliefs on the greater American public that is pushing this bill. I do not think the majority of gay people are for this. People like the log cabin republicans understand that it is not going to happen. Liberal groups like GLAAD and others need to sit down and shut up. I have nothing against people like Richard Simmons and Ellen Degeneris, because, for the most part, they just live their lives. They may speak out every now and then, but for the most part, they keep quiet. It's the Rosie O'Donnell's that get your goat.

Preacher Freedom
06/23/2007

Everybody needs to have freedom of speech. That includes priests, reverends, deacons, rabbis, and other who are supposed to be able to preach on anything. Frankly, I believe that being gay is a lifestyle and it is not genetic. The fact of the matter is this will be another way for the atheists to attempt to take religion out of everyday American life. We are supposed to have freedom of religion and the government is not supposed to to mandate a religion or any specific religion beliefs.

Things like this could kill the religion.

Closed Borders Means Things Will Get Better
06/24/2007

The big argument now is over the amnesty bill. I tend to believe that we should not do it the way the president wants to do it. There are certain groups wanting to pass this bill to amass power. When people on the wrong side of a bill are pushing a bill without a wall and do it in the back room, they want to keep it out of the light of day and from the eyes of the public. Some Latinos come here the right way and some are lazy and want to do it easy. They seek to cheat the system and sneak over the border.

That is wrong.

A wall would force the cheaters to enter this country the right way. There are always people who are going to cheat to get something for nothing. The wall would, also, cut down on the drug trade.

That is the deal.

Levee Boards Make You Say HMMM
06/25/2007

The number of the members on the Algiers/Jefferson Parish Levee Board causes a confusing convoluted problem.

It sounds like Algiers needs to have its own levee board and to be able to allocate its own money to help with fixing of their own levees. The people of Algiers want is due to them. The want the money they are supposed to have, in their hands.

If they continue to argue amongst themselves then outside entities may have to get involved to settle the problem.

"Bustberg'
06/26/2007

Michael Bloomberg is contemplating running for the presidency. This would have a detrimental effect on the ability of Hillary Clinton to get elected. Bloomberg is not a conservative.

Look at Bloomberg's record as mayor of New York City. he has done absolutely nothing of substance that was on the conservative side. He has raised taxes and pass useless laws. He passed a smoking ban and a trans-fat ban. Again, that is not conservative legislation.

He would be a "BUST" as a president.

Freedom Of Talk And Market Forces
06/29/2007

Life is a thing of balances. Balance in all things is good. Who's zooming who when the liberals say there is no balance for talk radio? Talk radio has everything from Hollywood to the New York Times. It can be argued that talk radio is balance. If the Fairness Doctrine is enacted, radio as we know it will die. It will take us back in time. Radio station will be forced to stop airing conservative talk radio.

The way this rule would work is that for every hour of conservative talk there must be an hour of liberal/progressive talk. The hope here is if it happens often enough the stations could decide to pull the conservative programming.

This is an entertainment based culture and even though politics is the topic it is still entertaining. It is a rating busines based on listeners and sponsors.

The Jim Hightower's, Air America, et al, did not have that "it". That "it" is a personality that is strong enough to transcend political affiliations. Even though people dislike Rush Limbaugh, he is entertaining enough for people on the other side of the isle to listen to him. Sean Hannity, Bill O'Reilley, Glenn Beck, Neal Boortz, and other that are in the local hosts/talent would be put out of jobs.

Let's look at what would happen to sports talk radio. If your favorite sports team is having a particularly bad season, then what? What would happen is that the particular team would be able to say that the fans could not hammer them and force the program off the air. It would allow them to do the same thing to sports hosts similar to the political hosts.

Iranian Build Up
07/01/2007

Mahmoud Adminidijahd is trying to build up the Iranian navy. We can not allow him to do this. If the navy becomes a strong one, then it would become even harder for the "coalition of the willing" to strike militarily. With a strong navy, Iran can patrol more area.

He is getting help from friends like Russia. He trades the oil for ships and other supplies. We not only need to address the Iran navy situation, but, also, need to confront those who enable Iran's causes

Real Reform
07/03/2007

Michelle Malkin has referred to the immigration bill as the "Shamnesty" bill. That is exactly what it is. They tried to push it through in the dark of night, in smoke filled rooms. That sounds like "Good Ole Boy" politics. They wanted to pass a bill that had not been fully written and, one the senators had read. Not only was the bill itself a sham, but so was the amendment process.

The hope is that the idiot politicians will get the message. The message is to get borders secure and then do the rest of the bill. Do it like any other bill, do each part of the bill in itself. That is the way the porcess should be done. When they tried to cobble it all together, they got to greedy. That is one particular time when greed was not good.

They need to do their jobs in the right way. As evident by the polls, they have not been doing the jobs very well.

Maybe, just maybe, they can get some real reform.

Another Country In the Coalition of The Willing
07/04/2007

Over the past ten to fifteen years Kosovo has been a tinderbox. It has been a haven for terrorists and they have been active in forestalling peace in the area. The leaders of the Kosovars are trying to get into the Europian Union which would help them, immensely, in rooting out the Albanian Jihadist terrorists.

After all, this is a global war on terror. We need all the help that we can get.

Turkish Trouble
07/05/2007

Could Turkey be in trouble going with Islam-O Fascism? The new president and foreign minister belong to a political party that believes in Islam-O-Fascism. They want a religious government. They are stepping back from and treaties and recognition of Israel. This could lead to one of the few democracies in the Middle East to go Islamist.

It could mean that it might become a haven for terrorists and their supporters. That is a dangerous thought.

Democrats Live Up To Their Mascot.
07/06/2007

The democrats are truly acting like their mascot. Their mascot is a donkey. They would like to get rid of the electoral college. That would not be wise and would be dangerous should a bad president gets in to office by the popular vote. The constitution states that we as a nation, do things the way, according to the law of the land.

At this point in time, we can't afford to listen to the crying democrats.

government, the one that was elected by a majority of the people. They are getting near to settling the whole oil profits issue.

In terms of the war, the Iraqi local leaders and Imams are getting tired of the infestations of terrorists that come from Al-Quaeda. They are not waiting for either coalition forces or Iraqi police forces; they are taking their freedom in their own hands. They are actually going out and killing the terrorists themselves.

Essentially, what Iraq has become is the "old west." In the old west the law could not be everywhere. What happen was that "Vigilance Squads" were formed. These consisted of normal people that got sick and tired of crime running rampant. These brave Iraqis are luring the terrorists to spots and setting off remote control road side bombs.

If we leave too soon, what will the Iraqi citizenry say and think? I do not know what they will say, but they will think the same thing that they thought when the job did not get finished during the first gulf war.

Water Money
07/15/2007

The majority of Louisianans can not quite wrap their minds aroundthe amount of money that is being spent on useless lakes and reservoirs. It is unfathomable to think about the amount of money being spent on new lakes and reservoirs while the ones we now have are not being care for. The majority of the $74,564,500 should be used to maintain the lakes that we have now. The question is: How do the lakes that will be built in other areas affect the economic impact in the area where Louisianans reside? The answer is that they don't.

The good people in Iberville are not getting any of the money. The people of the City of Plaquemine, have recently cleaned up Bayou Plaquemine and they did it by finding money themselves.

The state is doling out $41,534,500 and the good people of Iberville Parish will see none of that money. Do not get me wrong, I am glad we did not receive any of that money and I do not think that we need it. Even though we are not one of he richest parishes in the state, we did show any greed in asking for money for a useless project.

The plan is to spend $2.7 million dollars on the maintenance of all existing lakes and reservoirs. That is a definite good idea. I do think that they could spend more. It all goes back to the fact that it is like pulling teeth in trying to get the legislature to take care of state run buildings and facilities. Places like the PMAC (Pete Maravich Assembly Center), The River Center, Cajun Dome and others are in constant need of regular repair.

I will go back to the question:

Why do we need new lakes and reservoirs when we don't take care of the ones we have now?

Winning Costs Money
07/16/2007

If you are a sports fan you know that winning, for the most part, costs money. You have to be willing to spend money to get, keep, and retain players, coaches/managers, and front office personnel. The same is true for waging a war. It takes cash to pay for equipment, personnel and weapons to win any war. If we cut off the money we will lose the war. That is exactly what the democrats want.

I have said it before, Americans like to win and hate to lose.

His Spouse
07/17/2007

Some of the idiots on both sides of the isle are trying to make a big deal about Fred Thompson's age. Why should that matter? It should not. Yeah, his wife is 24 years younger than him; but it should not matter. One of our former presidents got married in the White House, and his wife was 15 to 20 years younger than him.

This is just another issue his opponents are trying to knock him down with.

Opportunity Knocks
07/20/2007

With the defeat of the amnesty bill there is an opportunity to get things right. In getting things right, I mean unite the party. To do that, first, you must build the wall and, then, work on the rest of the comprehensive amnesty bill.

Certain things in the amnesty bill need to be fine tuned. If the idiots in congress want it, they can fix it so that the wall and the enforcement provisions of the bill will work together. The green card/visa part of the bill needs to be changed. Here is how you might think about doing it:

1. Make big business buy the visas and green cards
2. Put the stipulation on the visa and green cards that said businesses must teach these people English
3. Put teeth in the background check part of the bill.
4. When building the fence make it high enough that it discourages people from climbing/jumping it
5. The last thing is to have a "virtual fence" which include:
    a) Using predator drones
    b) satellites
    c) robots
    6. Do not prosecute border agents for doing their jobs

That is just a few ideas that need to be infused into the bill for the ability of the bill to pass without the arousal of the same people that just defeated the bill in the first place.

Mike "MFP" Pasqua

What Kind of Governor Will We Get?
07/22/2007

The kind of governor we get in the next election, and the kind of governor we need is totally up to the Louisiana voters. We need a leader with a capital "L". A man or woman that is not afraid of going against the "Good Ole Boy" network. A person who is not afraid of doing the right thing even if it hurts him/her politically.

It is true that the person that eventually win the office will have a tough go of it, but, if he sticks to his guns, he can get the tough job done. Things like the Road Home Program and insurance need to be fixed. They need to curtail the perennial New Orleans crime rate. Fix the schools. Wean the state off of the money we are currently receiving for hurricanes Katrina and Rita.

That is going to be a tough job, but it is a job that has to be done.

No More New Deal For Farming
07/23/2007

The New Deal has killed a lot of things that were good about America. America's farms should be feeding the world, but they are not. The farm subsidies that were installed back then have lead to the current problems with the American agricultural system. It has lead to the creation and up-tick in the creation of corporate farms. That has really killed the family farm.

Senator Richard Lugar is right, when he says that things, in this respect, have to change. He wants American farms, once again, be great and be the backbone of this country.

It will be very hard for him to correct this problem because farming has become a big business. We need to go back to small business farming. We ought to let the farmers grow what they want and in whatever quantity they want. That's the way it was before the New Deal and that's the way it should be.

Benchmark This
07/24/2007

Putting such high benchmarks on the Iraqi government is wrong. That government is working at a snails pace, but it is working and it, in some respects, is working faster than the United States Government.

Congress needs to shut up and let the Iraqi government do their job. They are treating the Iraqis as a political football. We understand that the liberal kooks on the far left are running that party. We know what we get for them. We get high taxes, abortion, and welfare. Why can't they get it through their minds, they are making this a one party nation.

We know what they wanted to do with the Amnesty Bill is to add several million people to welfare roles; thereby, adding several million voters to the democratic rolls.

Such high benchmarks are wrong.

Quitting A Massacre
07/25/2007

When you were in school, playing a game, and you quit; What happened? There was a loss of respect for you in the schoolyard. Until you decided to play another game of the same sort and stick it out, win or lose, you would not get your respect back. You had to earn it back. The quitters in congress do not understand that if they continue on this bent, whatever respect we somehow accrued, will go up in smoke.

If we leave Iraq too soon, the horrors that would happen have been spoken of before and in great detail. As bad as it was during the reign of Sadam Hussein, it would be ten time worse if we left before finishing the job. To borrow a quote from pro wrestling, they need to "Know their role, and shut their mouth." Their role is to fund or not to fund the war and nothing else. The humanitarian abuses would be unprecedented. It would be like going back to the twelfth century. Don't even talk about the foreign policy disaster that would ensue. Public relations wise, the Islam-O-Fascists could and would claim a win. Reality wise, It would be another non-win for the military.

Basically, the liberals want another Vietnam.

Are We Ready For Romney
07/26/2007

Should we be phrasing the question another way? Usually a republican from a democrat state is a good thing. In terms of what is happening at this point in time, it could not hurt. I do not care about the man's religion, if he can get the job done he should be the next president. We got over our anti-Catholic sentiment when we elected President Kennedy.

The LDS can help in the protection of the country. Their extensive records of family genealogy can help keep to keep tract of the potential terrorists.

We flat out need to get over ourselves.

Time To Move On
07/27/2007

The people of Louisiana recently cried out for term limits. There are time that good things can be twisted. The way that the "Good Ole Boy" network twisted this good idea is they inserted a loophole that allows congresmen to jump form chamber to chamber. After twelve years they can go from the house to the senate and vise versa.

That is not the spirit of the law, but, it ishow the "Good Ole Boy" network operates. This is the reason the term limits will not change things.

West Bank Visit
07/28/2007

Recently of the a candidate that has high hopes in winning the governor' election made a visit to Iberville parish and to the city of Plaquemine. The biggest questions in my mind are:

1) How is he going to help Iberville Parish, which is one of the poorest parishes in the state, get better?

2) What is he going to do about taxes and "fees"?

3) Will he correct the Road Home Program?

4) We he be able to get the teachers a major pay raise?

5) How will he work around the "Good Ole Boy" network and the willing accomplices in the press?

Those are five big areas of importance. Especially number five. It will be made much easier if Bob Odom is sent packing to jail.

This recent visit to the west bank is a precursory visit to many more that will come to sure up this area.

Speed Kills But Not In Withdrawal
07/29/2007

In sports, it is said that speed kills. What this means is the faster a team is the harder it is to beat them. If America withdraws too fast it would be an incredible disaster. Politically, it would allow Iran to set up another "satellite" nation. That would facilitate a greater attack on Israel, not to mention the fact, that it would allow Al-Qaeda to get set up and to reconstitute their command hierarchy.

It would be one less nation on our side.

Air Delay
07/30/2007

Recently a HB 841 came up. This is the bill for the new cargo airport in the Donaldsonville area. It got killed by some representatives for unknown reasons.

With all of the business and residential growth in the area we cannot understand why this bill was killed.

What is even worse is that the persons who killed it will not tell the public why. The public deserves to know why they are letting pettiness get in the way of the area and the state making another step forward in getting out from the history of its bad business climate.

We have projects popping up like a possible loop, a land based casino, Bass Pro Shops, Cabela's, and others. Cities are cleaning themselves up and growing at pretty good rates. Why would they want to stop this business venture that would impact the entire west-bank area, from Baton Rouge to New Orleans?

Is it a case of greed?

We just don't know.

Safety Games
07/31/2007

The democrats are playing games with the safety of the American people. They are trying to make it so that people will not report suspicious behavior that occurs on airliners. This stems from the flying Imams story. Those particular guys were acting very peculiar and the patrons of the flight got very afraid.

The democrats are so beholden to political correctness and the trial lawyers that represent people who try to harm others and harm this country. This is just another way for these lawyers to make money.

My big question is just how will this affect the Crime Stoppers program and America's Most Wanted.

A Fistful Of Vetoes
08/01/2007

Recently, lame duck Governor Kathleen Babineaux "What's Her Face" Blanco vetoed five tax bills. According to a bipartisan majority in the legislature, these tax breaks would help a new day dawn in the state of Louisiana. The tax breaks would, not only help the state attract big business, but it would also help the Moms and Pops to remain in business.

Why would she do this? She is on her way out of office. This is just another mistake in a long line of mistakes that she has made. It has been proven she is not very politically astute. Why is she still beholden to the teachers union? After all, she is not running for reelection, Is she not?

Airport Response
08/02/2007

State Representative Roy Quisere took his ball and went home over the bill that would have increased the power of the Louisiana Airport Authority. It would have made public some, so called, "sensitive" documents. What he does not understand is when it is a government subsidiary it becomes the public's right to know information; because it is the public's money that will be spent to complete the project. Even though the project will benefit the whole state, the people still need to know it.

I am so proud of Representative Rob Marionneaux for killing the bill because it was the right thing to do. That does not mean that the bill can not be brought back in the next session. It also means problems with the bill can be corrected.

Frankly, I think that he (Quisere) got greedy.

Back Door
08/03/2007

Our much "Esteemed" Governor Kathleen Babineaux "What's Her Face" Blanco recently vetoed a bill that would have given an income tax break to those families that choose to send their children to private or parochial schools.

We all know that she is beholden to the teachers unions and that is one of the reasons for a veto of the bill. I do not understand why she is still beholden to the unions. The is only one reasons I can see why she would do this. She may be planning to change her mind on the issue of running for the office of the governor.

The teachers think that it would kill the public schools. It might very well do that; but I tend to lean the other way. I will go even farther than that and say the vouchers are sorely needed.

The teachers are afraid that the bad teachers will be weeded out. That sounds like a good idea to me.

Long Term
08/04/2007

Most people like to protect their investments. We, as a nation, need to protect the investment we made in Iraq and we will make in Iran. It will be just like what we did at the end of World War II, when we built Ramstien Air Base.

Whey a country invests so much in trying to protect itself, then why not go whole hog in doing this. We are going to build a brand spanking new imbassy and air base. The embassy will be on a tract of land the size of 80 football fields. The air base will be on a 15 square mile piece of land. Both will be like mini cities. At the current air base (Balad) all of the equipment and supplies for the troops are dispersed.

If we (U.S.) are going to have a long term military presence in the middle east we need these two thing to be up and running and soon.

Turnout?
08/05/2007

In most cases, turnout is the key to a particular election. In the case of the recent tax election to vote on a tax for teachers and for up-keep of the school buildings in Iberville Parish, it was not the key. It was lack of turn out. Because the tax election was the only issue to be voted on, those person having a keen interest in the school system got out and voted. Most of those who cast ballots voted for the tax. The turn-out was very low

The supportors of the tax feared if over fifty percent of the voters shows up on election day the tax would not passed. That is a great lack of confidence in the voter.

If the majority of the voter in the parish wished for the tax not to pass, they should have made it a priority to get-out-and vote.

Transportation Center
08/06/2007

There are 25,000 acres of land that ten communities want to turn into an intermodal transportation center. This would not only help those ten comminutes, but it would also help all of the others in the area.

This is not just the cargo airport but it also railroads, and waterways. It would help more businesses like Cabela's and Bass Pro to move into the area.

All in all, it would be a good idea for the area.

Corps Of Rhetoric
08/07/2007

The Army Corps of Engineers is getting to be a political entity. It is not known why they are refusing to build the levees in the New Orleans/Southeast Louisiana levees to the level they can protect those particular areas from a category five hurricane and its storm surge.

The Corps claims that it would cost too much money to do that. Would it not cost even more money if there was another storm of the century and the same thing happened? I think that it would.

While they are at it, the Corps should build the protection above and beyond for added protection. It would definitely improve their image with the people of New Orleans.

Political Weekend Golf
08/08/2007

In golf, there is a term for the weekend /bad golfers, and it is the word is "hacker". This means that they do not hit fairways, miss the greens, and putt poorly. Also, in computer terms, the work hacker is generally a bad thing. It is a person that breaks into the files of a computer of another person to steal information.

The governor has ramped her political hack in and out of the legislature not to go into a special session to override her recent vetoes on some very important tax bills. The hacks in the legislature are the same ones that believe that lakes and reservoirs are economic developments. Her hacks outside the legislature are the sycophants that elected her and she keeps breaking her promises and make bad decisons, especially on tax issues.

It all goes back top. The fact that the "Good Ole Boy" n etwork just do not want the state to get better and move on to better things.

No-Ethics Board
08/09/2007

This, as I term it, "No-Ethics Board" is at it again. It refuses to enforce the ethics rules on the government, but it is going to do it against state employees. The employees are the people that run the Louisiana Community and Technical College System. They were brought to Lake Jackson, Texas, to observe a program on industrial training. According to Dow this would help to elivate the technical and industrial ability of the Louisiana workforce.

They (No-Ethics Board) are fitting very nicely with the rest of the state government that has hurt this fair state for the last forty years.

Got Your Ethics Right Here
08/10/2007

Ethics in American politics, in local, state, and national government, is sorely lacking. We have pork flying all over the place. What is scary is that when a group of people come along that want to correct the problem the sycophants try as hard as possible to stop it. Then, there are the unethical law makers who use words to pass laws to stymie the correction of the problem.

When you got people, in all facets of government, that all they want is the pork, you can understand how all of the good things that need to be done do not get done.

Political ethics is needed in all areas of the government and it needs to be fixed. It is as simple of that.

Poor Business Climate
08/11/2007

According to Forbes Magazine, Louisiana is ranked forty-ninth in the nation in all parts of the business community. We are one of the poorest states in the union. We know that we have businesses that are moving out of the state and do not plan to come back. Things definitely needs to change. We need to encourage business, not only to move here, but to stay here.

Some people will never-ever understand that when you cut taxes, you help the business community. When taxes are cut, it encourages businesses to invest in equipment and personnel, and growth. It also helps other business that do not currently reside in your state. It helps business everywhere.

In terms of this state and its business community, the governor is stuck on stupid.

Al-Qaeda In Iran More Than An Estimate
08/12/2007

The National Intelligence Estimate (NIE) states, with no uncertainty, that Al-Qaeda is definitely in Iran planning attacks on the Iranian people. They (Al-Quaeda) also want to attack America.

Al-Qaeda holds high level meetings in eastern part of Iran and in Pakistan.

The presidents' of Pakistan and Afghanistan should take a tougher stand in their fight with the terrorist. The Pakistani president needs to stop making deals with these people and just to kill them. The United States needs to support them in all of their efforts.

Climbing Over 'Katrina' Mary
08/13/2007

As much as the democrats and her election campaign may say it is not so, Senator Mary Landreiu is in trouble. With her base in New Orleans gone, I think it will be, incredibly, hard for her to get reelected. The voters that would vote for her are gone, and, also the people that could help her cheat to win the election are gone, too. The Hispanic minority rules New Orleans right now, and for the most part they are not citizens. This means that they can not vote. The democrat mayor of the city, who is not a friend of the Landreiu's, had to depend on the white people in the city to get reelected. For the most part, the white peiople in the city, democrats or republicans, are conservative. The votes that she lost in New Orleans, she must get someplace else. That is going to be a chore, because for he most part, in the rest of the state her last two elections were close.

As in everything with her, it will all come down to New Orleans. The question is:

How many dead people will end up voting?

Shintech Is Good For Iberville
08/14/2007

Shintech appears to be one of the few things that Governor "What's Her Face" Blanco has done. Because of the ties that the company has to the governor, it appeared to be a political deal. On the whole it was a very good "get". It helped get some jobs into the state. It also helped to get people to move into Iberville parish and into the Plaqemine area.

As of August 10, 2007, plans are being made to add more facilities to what they have already built at Shintech. This means even more jobs and economic development for this area.

Every little bit that anyone can do will help the area to develop economically.

The is not what the people had in mind. This is just one reason why this is such an important election.

Fleischman, Another Reason To Fight Against The Fairness Doctrine
08/23/2007

Jon Fleischman, a republican blogger, is a very powerful person in California and in the national republican party. Blogging is a way to allows normal people to apply more political pressure on lawmakers. This person Fleischman, helped to defeat the very bad Immigration Bill.

The democrats have said that they want to bring back the Fairness Doctrine. They want to shut down the alternative media. The democrats think, and rightly so, that talk radio, Fox News, and the internet hurt them when they attempt to pass laws. Fleischman, Limbaugh, Hannity, yours truly, and the like, are the people that the Fairness Doctrine is aimed towards.

If the liberals wanted true fairness, when they look at talk radio and the internet then they should, also, look at the mainstream (ABC, NBC, CBS, CNN, MSNBC, The New York Times, The Chicago Sun Times, The LA Times, et all.) media; and look at the way they report their stories.

War Of Words
08/25/2007

John and Elizabeth Edwards, who wants to be the president and the first lady, really should not be getting into a war of words with a political commentator. This shows that someone can get under his skin and at times he can be a real hot head. Obama and Clinton ignore the majority of commentators on both side of the isle. The media can really elect or try to elect a president, but for the most part, it does not happen that way. If Edwards lets himself get baited by the press, what is going to happen when should he get into high level negotiations with other heads of state.

Changes In Party Politics
08/26/2007

The republican party of Louisiana wants to go to a closed primary system for their elections of their U.S. Senate and U.S. House of Representative seats. Until this time, anyone could vote in the Republican primary. I think that for a time, that was a good idea. The reason it has been this way was for a long time it was very hard for any republican to get elected in the state of Louisiana. Sure, Dave Treen got elected in 1979, but since then it has been slim pickings. You really should not count the politicians that switched parties recently because if you look at their voting records, they would be considered no better than rhinos.

The Report Is In
08/27/2007

In 1948, President Truman created the National Petroleum Council to represent the oil industry. One of their reports stated what it will take for America to have energy independence. They said that we need to combine all types of energy. We need to get every drop of oil out of the earth that we can. There needs to more refineries built. The bio fuels sector needs to get stronger and more proactive. There needs to be a way for someone to figure how to lower the production cost of ethanol. Suffice to say, that we need to build more nuclear power plants. Coal is another energy source that we have to get to get it from the ground. In the case of solar and wind base energy, there needs to be a push to make it more feasible. The people like the Kennedy's need to get it through their thick sculls that wind farms will help their immediate community.

What really needs to happen is that we, as a country, need to tell the environmental wack-o's to take a flying leap.

Young Rebuilders
08/28/2007

It seems that the twenty-somethings are helping to rebuild New Orleans. The entrepreneurial spirit is alive and well in the "Big Easy". Young people are moving into the city in droves and may be the engines that will help the city to recover. These twenty-somethings are starting all kinds of businesses, both for profit and not-for-profit. Sure, there may be some carpet baggers, but for the most part, they are moving there to stay and put down long term roots. It sure helps that the pro sports teams are populated with that same age group. With Reggie Bush, Drew Brees, and Chris Paul and all of their high profile teammates, twenty-somethings is going strong.

This city is getting back to something close to what it was in the past. Keep going.

Thick Skulls
08/29/2007

The democrats are beating their heads on a brick wall and do not seem to be getting a head injury. They need to get it into their heads that we are not coming out Iraq until Bush leaves office. In the next millennia when they dig for bones, they will see certain skull that are unusually thick. When they see these thick skulls they will assume these were democrats. They, then, can assume they were the skulls of dummies.

Days On Patrol
08/31/2007

When the coalition now go on patrol, especially in parts of Iraq's battle zone, the fierce fighting is no longer there. As far as the soldier are concerned, that is just fine. The Iraqi general public, unlike the democrat party, loves the American military. There is still a wary optimism on the a great change in the legislature and we will have a reform minded governor. Also, with this change, there is a good chance that this state will go completely to the republicans.

The "Good Old Boy" network is in trouble. When they get in trouble, they attack. They are making a vicious attack on Kennedy's beliefs and character. This is a good man who has done a very good job as the Secretary of State of the State of Louisiana.

Welcome To The Party
09/09/2007

John Kennedy has defected to the republican party. I say welcome. Over the time he has been in office, he has been acting more like a republican than a democrat; and it is about time that he made the switch.

The man is a classy person who deserves to be in the republican party. He will help make this state one of the best in the Union.

The democrats are crying over spilled milk. The should have read between the lines and saw it coming. They are trying to take their ball and go home. This should not surprise anyone because they do this every time they lose on any big issue. It is like Rush Limbaugh says "They are opening the door right on their noses."

Staying Power While Staying In Power
09/11/2007

Our military power, no matter how many people do not like it, must stay right where it is. If we do not stay put, then who will. As of now there is no other "power" in the world with the where-with-all of military or money to get the job done. We are it. If we leave, the European Union and it's member countries would be the first freedom loving countries that would be hit with terrorism and the EU knows it. That is why the new Prime Minister of Britain did an about face when he got into office. You could say the same thing with Angela Merkel (Germany) and Nicolas Sarkozy (France). The European leaders have to pay lip service at face value to the liberal anti-war groups but behind closed doors and in the back channels, they are staunchly behind Americans in, whatever they do.

We Are Winning, To Some Extent
09/12/2007

In Iraq, the war is being won if the idiots in Washington allow it to be won. If you have been over there and have talked to the boots on the ground, they say as much. As of this time, there is no civil war. Could there be? Yes, if we leave too soon. Have we turned some of the problem spots around? Yes. Could they go back? Yes. Will they go back? Yes and No. Yes, if we leave to soon. No, if we stay and finish the job. We should not turn 2007 into 1975.

We are winning the military part of the war, if the Iraqi government would cooperate. My hope is that the Iraqi people will get fed up and change their national government.

Ties to Edwards Could Be Gone; Or At Least Have Less Power
09/13/2007

With John Alario in office, the good "Good Ole Boy" network is in force. He needs to go. If he remains in the senate and the democrats retain the senate there will not be the reform this state sorely needs. Alario is one of the people that has ties to former governor (and currently incarcerated) Edwin W. Edwards. He needs to stay in jail and Alario needs to be out of office.

Alario is one of the most crooked and egregious offenders of ethics law. If the people can find the testicular fortitude to elect someone different there will be great changes in the state. Here is something else to think about. There is the need of six other seats than his to change. If the democrats lose those six seats then Alerio's election might not matter.

Does The Black Caucus Really Represent Black Louisianans?
09/19/2007

The Louisiana Black Caucus, much like the National Black Caucus, is a very liberal organization. There is a real question on whether they really represent a majority of the African-American Louisiana population. For the most part, they are hard working and even though the majority of the blacks are democrats, they may be of the "Blue Dog" variety.

The bill that got passed states that one must show identification to prove he or she is who they say they are so that they can vote. I would assume that most African Americans have a social security card, driver's license, or other forms of identifications that would allow them to prove themselves for the ability to vote. The question is. Do we really care what the Louisiana Black Caucus thinks?

Why So Many
09/20/2007

In this up coming governor's election there are many (9) candidates. The majority of these candidates probably do not have a chance to win. There are a couple of them that have serious ties to former governor, Edwin W. Edwards, and want him out of jail. Those people should not be seriously considered because of the fact that if Edwards gets out, it would not help the state's image. Any moves back to corruption, no matter how small, would automatically be bad for our state.

There are only three real candidates. They are Bobby Jandal, Walter Boasso, and Foster Campbell. Governor "What's Her Face" Blanco has effectively killed the ability of any woman, at least for the next two elections, to be the governor of the state.

Suffice it to say, that I think that Jindal will be the next governor of this fair state.

The V-Word Could End Up In Death For The Democrats
09/21/2007

Any war that come to the forefront right now the liberal side of the democrat party will be against it. The reason is that the "kook fringes" of their party is where the money is and they are against any war, no matter how just. They compare it to Vietnam. Each and ever war is a different entity in and of themselves.

If they do not be careful, this next election will end up like the second elections of Nixon and Reagan. Those elections were, essentially, big blow outs for the republican. The reason why this happened was that the majority of Americans like to win and they just do not see the democrats as the party that wants the country to be a winner in anything.

Odom's Fear
09/22/2007

Louisiana State Agricultural Commissioner Bob Odom needs to go. He is one of the former governor Edwin W. Edwards holdovers. This man is corrupt and he is a crook. He is drunk with power and we have some yellow-bellied, lily-livered, politicians in the state legislature that will not tell him no. The last several governors have also been afraid of him. Any bill, measure, tax, or fee that he wants passed will get passed. Any idea that come from his black heart and evil mind will become a bill and eventually a law. He dreadfully misuses that office and has done so since he first got elected.

Flat out , the man needs to go.

Hsu Gives Term "Wide Left" A New Look
09/23/2007

The crooked fund raiser Norman Hsu's contact were far reaching. The people he bilked out of money are the innocents. He was masquerading as a legitimate fund raiser and he even fooled the Democratic Legislative Committee. Hillary Clinton is as stupid as she is crooked for allowing Hsu to get as close to her as he did.

This is just another reason that she does not belong in the highest office in the land.

In Trouble?
09/24/2007

As the democrats continue to open the door right on their noses, this could lead to them losing the slim majority that they have. If, whomever, ends up as the democrats nominee tries to move to the center, what will happen is the "Move On's" and the liberal blogs will savage them. They will cut the funds for the election of the eventual president.

What needs to happen on the republican side is to have the party unite under whomever is the nominee. It could be a conservative; it could be Rudy Giuliani. The conservatives need to have a person who is strong on defense, taxes, and social issues. Is it possible for the republicans to win on two of three of those issues? Yes, and it would greatly increase the likelihood of the nominee winning the president's office if he would be strong on all of those issues.

Back on the democratic side, they need to be as liberal as possible or they will not have a shot. The liberals want people to promote the ideals that they believe in. The far-left kooks do not get that the majority of the country, on both side of the isle, are conservative. The problem is that the far-left kooks are ruling the democratic party. If their candidates can not step away from the far-left kooks they will have a very big defeat.

Comments Smell.
9/25/2007

Barry Manilow dropped his appearance on The View because of Elizabeth Haselbeck's views. On the face of the comment, one would say that he has the right to do that. You must look deeper. If you did look deeper you would see that Rosie O'Donnell is helping to promote and appear, in some part, on his record. This was just another way Rosie was able to try to get over on Elizabeth.

It now appears that Rosie is trying to get other famous persons to do her dirty work.

Jersey Boys Are Indicative Of All Of The Armed Forces
09/26/2007

The brave people who make up the armed forces are the positive persons about the war in Iraq. There is no group that embodies this more than the 1st platoon, 2nd Battalion, Fox Company Marines. The majority of this group is from New Jersey and they want to stay in Iraq until the job is done, no matter how much time it takes. I would wager to say that they are making their grandparents and great-grandparents very proud. The afore-mentioned grandparents and great-grandparents were the ones that were in the "Greatest Generation." They all agree, uniformly, there is still some work to do and that it is better for them to be there and keeping us safe then for them to be home and terrorist attacks happening on the U.S. homeland.

Is Anti-Semitism Alive And Well
09/27/2007

We all know that Anti-Semitism is a horrid thing, and it is alive and well. There are two academics that are "trying to pry the lid" off of a particular debate they are saying has been festering for decades. In their mind, is the question of whether the Israeli lobby is too strong. My feelings are that this particular lobby is as strong as it needs to be. If it were not for Israel we might not have any friends at all.

Seriously, these two academics sound like they are anti-Semitic.

A Democratic Lebanon Is A Must
09/28/2007

The majority of the world wants an independent and democratic Lebanon. Syria and Iran do not. We know that Iran wants as many friends and puppet states as they possibly can have. They want to accrue as much power in the region as they can possibly can get. If Lebanon can stay free, then that is another possible friend for the United States in the war on terror in that region.

Iran has long sought to sabotage any move towards democracy in the middle east. They know if it continues, they will have been surrounded on all sides by free and democractic nations. It would appear seeing what their neighbors have, the Iranian people would also want freedom. Freedom and democracy breeds freedom and democracy.

Pelican Vice
09/29/2007

In the 1980's there was a television show called Miami Vice. It starred Don Johnson. As of right now, in Louisiana, there are multiple ethics investigations going on that we can now call "Pelican Vice." We are trying to clean up our image but it does not help that there are people that do not have the moral fiber to act in the right way. Judge Don Johnson has allowed himself to fall in with the corrupt, unscurrilous, unethical people. We know the history of Both BobOdom and Cleo Fields. It is not arguable that they are not ethical and they do not apologize for what they do.

France's Ronald Reagan
09/30/2007

Nicolas Sarkozy wants to drag France and Europe in a different direction. This man appears to be the French equivalent to Ronald Reagan. He, it appears, is putting together a very conservative progressive agenda. He wants France to have stronger relations with America. He wants to return to NATO's ruling body. He wants to have a strong military. He sees the danger in Iran having nuclear weapons. Those are just a handful of issues that he feels strong about.

This man could be the next great European leader.

Secret Plan
10/01/2007

News is slowly leaking out of Washington D.C. about a possible attack on Iran. It is no surprise that they are trickling out, but what is surprising, is the joint chiefs are putting together, what could be better, more detailed plans in secret. We, as the American people, will not know what the exact plans are until they are executed.

The first part of the plan should be a counter-information campaign. Part of that campaign should be sending people into the colleges and universities in Iran. The students and professors seem to be willing to be used in that way. Those two groups of people look to have the guts to create a possible Tiananmen Square incident. What that would do would put "President" Ahmadinejad and the Mullahs in a position to look even worse than they already do. If a massive protest, that includes the incredibly young and the intellectual elites, would create an uprising, it would force the mlitary to be called out. If that happens there could be a Tiananmen Square feel to it.

That is just part of it. What also needs to be done is for special operaations to go in and to destroy Iran's only oil refinery.

If none of that works, then we have no choice but to go to war.

Don't Do It
10/02/2007

Former presidential candidate Gary Hart recently gave the Iranians a fair warning. The warning is to tone down rhetoric and actions, if they wished not to be attacked. If the Mullahs were smart people they would call Ahminedijad in and put a muzzle on him. They may have the same goals, but if President Tom keeps shooting off his mouth then the King Kong/Godzilla of the world will come in a wreak total and irrevocable destruction on a proud society. The "nut bag" that is the president of Iran just does not get it. He will not shut up. If he would just keep his mouth closed, then there is a possibility they could do what they want to do in secret.

Why Are Jews Liberal
10/03/2007

The answer to the question:

Why are American Jews Liberal?

One has to go back to World War II. Much like the Europeans, this current Jewish generation is liberal because that is the political leaning of the president, Franklin D. Roosevelt, and the party that was in power at the time. If a conservative was in power at that time, they would be conservative. Those are the facts.

Can this change? Yes. Will it change? I don't know. If parents raised their children in that way of thought, then it will not change. But, if the parents are more open minded then there will be a precipitous change.

Myanmar Freedom
10/04/2007

The monks in Myanmar (Burma) are marching for more freedom. The human psyche urns for freedom. Freedom is the natural state of the human psyche. All the people in all of the repressed countries want freedom but somehow they do not have the strength of character and means/

ability to get the job done. The Burmese government should be careful because if they come on too strong there will be repercussions. The rest of the world will not stand for it.

Why We Are Winning
10/05/2007

As of this point in time, we are winning in Iraq. The surge is working. The Iraqi general population is getting involved in the protection of their country. The Iraqis see the commitment to root out the people that are terrorizing them and are now joining in. They are sick and tired of being sick and tired. They want to be free and have democracy that fits them. They see that the terrorists are threating them and they are now willing to come out and fight for it.

Yes, their national government is less that efficient, but that is no different than how the majority of democratic national governments got started. The local warlords, tribal leaders, and religious leaders are doing their jobs spectacularly. They are doing an incredible job of rallying the general public to the cause. Up until a couple of months ago, that just did not happen.

Mr. Bag-O-Cash Can't Run
10/06/2007

The Louisiana Supreme Court recently returned a decision that stated that Cleo Fields, the Louisiana Stat Legislator, famous for accepting bribes in bags, could no longer run for the legislature. Thank, The Lord! This is another Edwin W. Edwards guy that needed to go. He has been in Baton Rouge for a very long time. His votes have, for the most part, hurt the state.

After the ruling, he came out and endorsed Mrs. Yvonne Dorsey. I do not know why any democratic politician would accept his endorsement of Fields. If she wants to appear that she is not corrupt she should not accept it. It is going to make it incredibly hard for her to get elected because if she aleigns herself with Fields.

Ulrich Could Educationally Improve Louisiana's Students
10/07/2007

Ruth Ulrich, whom this blogger listened and talked to, could be one of the best changes that could happen in the upcoming election. She has some interesting ideas on how to retool, and update the Louisiana BESE Board. The BESE Board is just another institute in this state that has gotten bogged down in Louisiana politics. It appears that the BESE board has been mired in the past and has not wanted to be updated. Much like the rest of the state, the board may have to be dragged, kicking and screaming into the future.

Mrs. Ulrich has stated that there should be more accountability. Accountability would assure that the per student money is spent in the right places and in the right ways.

She wants high school redesign. She would like to see vocational education put back into the schools. That would spur the people less likely to go to college, to acquire the skills necessary to be successful and to apply those skills within the state. This would definitely help economic development.

If a students needs are not being met and that student is not doing well, that student should be allowed to find a place at which he or she can be successful. If that is a charter, private, or parochial school, then so be it.

I, also, agree that we need to get rid of the incompetent teachers. If those teachers can be weeded out then the educational level of all students will rise.

Confidence Lacking
10/08/2007

The Louisiana Democratic Party's confidence looks to be sorely lacking and rightly so. The feeling one gets is that there is a great deal of change coming in this state. The democrats, who have been in power for over one hundred years, have the most to lose. If the bad politicians get voted out the bad politics go with them. Things like claiming economic development where there is none, and redefining words that do not need to be redefined. It can be said that the majority of the current legislature have some ties to former governor, Edwin W. Edwards. We all know how crooked Edwards was. I may be painting with a big, broad brush but I do think we are in for drastic changes in this upcoming election. We have seen present legislators buy golf courses that the state should not own, build lakes that should not be built, and do other nefarious things that should not be done. They have killed bills that should have been laws and passed laws that should not have been passed.

Flat out, the confidence is not there.

Distraction
10/09/2007

The current, ongoing flap over Rush Limbaugh's "Phoney Soldier" comment is the latest in a long line of distractions by the liberals. This is designed to draw attention away from the Nancy Pelosi/HarryReid lead congress that has been an abject failure. Because they can not get their agenda passed, they are trying everything to divert the public's attention away from their failures. All of the little nit picking things that they have tried to get to stick to the president have slid away like a child on a Slip-N-Slide. They do not have the power to impeach. They do not have the power to override a veto. They do not have the power to end the war and, frankly, in the back of their minds, I do not think they want to end it.

Any distraction that they can come up with, they will try.

Big Easy Debate
10/11/2007

Is appears that the Louisiana Recovery Authority, is lobbying the Commission on Presidential Debates to have a debate in New Orleans. I agree it would help the city in its recovery. It would be just another way to show that New Orleans is open for business.

New Orleans, before the storm, was known as one of the best convention cities in the nation. Annually, it was on the top of the list of cities bests suited to have conventions, concerts, and other shows. This would be another way to reestablish the cities standing in that area. The president election is the hiring process for the most important job in the nation, if not the world. This would be another step in the slow march back to what was one of the greatest, historical cities in the world.

Odom Needs To Go
10/13/2007

Bob Odom, one of the most corrupt and unscrupulous politicians in the history of Louisiana, needs to be ousted from office. For nearly thirty years, he has given this state a giant black eye. He has made people not only look weak on paper but appear weak in truth. If he does not want your bill to go through the legislature he will use his influence to make sure it will not see the light of day. He is a con man of the highest order. He can talk governors out of signing bills that would be good for the state and a boom to its people. He is still closely tied to former governor, Edwin Edwards. As of this point-in-time, he is the top power broker of the democratic side in the state.

Can any of the other candidates that are running against him beat him? I hope so.

Will he pull out all of the stops and dirty tricks to win? You know he will.

Can he be beaten? Yes.

Will he be beaten? We will just have to wait and see.

Challenge
10/14/2007

Mitch Landrieu, much like his older sister "Katrina" Mary, is in trouble. It all started in the last election when he could not win the mayor's race for the city of New Orleans. Now he has four serious challengers for the office of lieutenant governor. He has not done very much in office. There are certain things that he has direct power over and he has not used that power. He could have done a better job in the promotion of the state.

His four opponents are Gary Beard (R-Baton Rouge), Sammy Kershaw (R-Laffayette), Thomas Kates (I-Bogolusa), and Norris "Spanky" Gros Jr. (I-Pierre Part). Beard wants an air network that would connect the largest cities in the state with each other to eliminate the need to fly outside the state to go from New Orleans to Baton Rouge. Kates wants to resend the tax credits that were given to the movie industry. Kershaw wants to promote the state and its culture. I think that he can get the job done because he has had experience in promotion.

I like Kershaw.

After Reagan's Heart
10/15/2007

Bobby Jindal is a man after Ronald Reagan's heart. He is a conservative with a positive outlook and thinks that he can do a lot of good in correcting the problems of this state. I tend to believe him. He was elected to the House of Representatives and has done the job that the people of Louisiana has hired him to do. What he says and how he is saying it is attracting people like a moth to a flame.

The other side of the isle is deathly afraid of Jindel, and it shows. They are trying to take him down but I do not think that the vast majority of the people in the state are buying it. He is an imminently likeable man.

More Seats
10/16/2007

Because of illegal immigration, certain states will get a chance to receive more congressional seats. When the census takes place, in 2010, the states with the most illegal immigrants will get an increased number of sitting representatives and senators.

What should happen, is that if a person is an illegal immigrant, he should not be counted in the census. If one has come to this country illegally, he should not be counted as a citizen of this country. The census needs to be tweaked but it will not happen with the democrats in charge. Those illegal immigrants are potential voters. Everything with the democrats is political and power based.

Electable Women
10/17/2007

Women are getting elected to high offices all over the world at an increasing rate. Let us look at Argentina and Pakistan. In Pakistan, the current president is in trouble and my lose to Mrs. Bhutto. In Argentina the wife of the current president is running. This lady was a senator before her husband decided to get into politics. As her husband was serving as president the question was asked:

Why is she not running for the office? She would be a better leader than him.

Freedom Creeps Slowly In Iran
10/19/2007

Slowly, but surely, freedom is coming to Iran. Iraian women are not only owning businesses, but they are also able to dress like western women. To that extent, the amount of women having plastic surgery is up. They want everything from botox to breast enhancement. They just want to look good. This is an exercise in vanity. In this case it is good because if the leaders crack down on the women, they might have an uprising that would be very hard to control. The western world wants, so much, for these women to succeed.

Will We Change
10/20/2007

Today is election day. This is a day that could hold much promise for the state of Louisiana. The fact of the matter is that for the last forty years we, as a state, have been on a downward spiral and the politicians we have selected have not done anything to correct and improve the situation. We, as a state, have been living under Murphy's Law. This states that whatever can go wrong, will go wrong. Even if some things have been corrected for the good, that did not mean they would stay corrected. More often than not, things would not be corrected, and the state has continued to get worse.

I think, that thanks to the two hurricanes of a couple of years ago, we have had enough of the same old, same old. I think that we are about ready to stand up as one state and say "NO MORE!". We are about to give the Bob Odom, John Alario, Francis Heitmeier, and the rest of the corrupted liberal democrats a collective "up yours". We will get out the biggest broom that we can find and sweep all of them away. It is going to be a political Katrina and they will all get blown away and flooded out.

No Break
10/21/2007

The conservative Christians who want to break with the conservative party, because they do not want to trust any of the candidates for president, are not very smart. It is very difficult to understand what a Hillary Clinton presidential reign would do to our country. The Supreme Court justices that are liberal are getting close to retirement. Should Clinton get elected, she would have more than one appointment to make to the bench. This would make the court lean more the the side of the liberal democrats. What we would like to see is a more conservative candidate get elected, thus slanting the opinions of the court more to the thinking of the majority of the people of this country. If we can get this more conservative Supreme Court, the national abortion laws could go by the boards and be sent back to the individual states. Things like Gay marriage and parental notification would be on the fast track to becoming law.

Most of the people who are unhappy with the current crop of republican candidates need to understand the pragmatic results of a Hillary presidency.

Delusional
10/22/2007

Scott Ritter and the others who think that there is no reason to go into Iran are wrong. It has been proven that the Iranian government wants to develop and use nuclear weapons. From top to bottom, they are one on the most oppressive regimes in the world. What is even worse about this government, is that they will, from time to time, give their people freedom only to, later, take it away. They are a state sanctioner of terrorism. We know exactly where they stand on Israel. Their "President" has all but said that the Iranian leadership wants Israel to be done away with. Going into Iraq was all about Iran. We wanted to use President Theodore Roosevelt's theory of "Speak softly, and carry a big stick." We needed to show Iran what happens to people that mess with America.

A Democrat Is A Democrat
10/23/2007

Leopards do not change their stripes and neither do democrats. A democrat now is the same as a democrat in 1864. Both sets are and were anti-war and the two groups are just a bit racist. In 1864, the civil war was not going well and the democrats wanted out. The reports from the front lines were massive amounts of casualties and "atrocities" committed in the fog of war. What was understood was that once Atlanta fell public sentiment changed. Why the sentiment change? The north was beginning to win the war. American people like to win. Because of this turning of the war, Abraham Lincoln got reelected.

The three top democrat candidates for president are walking back from their promise to totally withdraw from Iraq. They are understanding that this particular position is a losing one in the general election. They could actually be a very big loser in the next election. It could not only cost them the White House bus also the congress. If they do not watch out they could lose whatever power that they think they have.

Youth Be Served
10/23/2007

Bobby Jindal is the youngest governor in the nation. In the business of Louisiana politics, you almost have to a young man or woman to get serious things done. Bobby Jindal is 36 years old and he is the first person of color that has won this governor's seat since reconstruction.

He has boundless energy, that will translate into the ability to get thing done and take this state in a positive direction.

Rock Solid Standing
10/24/2007

The GOP of Louisiana may very well be on their way to getting a firm grip on Louisiana. We will see, much like the national party, if they do not "lose their way." They must hold strong to their conservative beliefs. They must not go on a spending spree. They have to keep their promises about getting rid of the income taxes. Most important of all, they can not pass bad bills that would obviously hurt this fair state. If they can follow this platform and abide by the rule of term limits, they party could be in power for a long time.

Let's see what happens.

Family Pride
10/25/2007

Bobby Jindal's family is proud of him, and rightly so. The man has achieved so much at such a young age. Anytime some one as young as he accomplishes these goals he is automatically said to be a rising star. This man has potential off of the charts. Right now, he is aspiring to correct the problems in this state. Later on, he might be consider to be "The Leader Of The Free World."

We will see where Jindal's ability and ambition takes him.

Big Discussion
10/26/2007

Rudy Guiliani may be the Republican nominee for the office of The President of the United States. If he becomes the nominee, there could be a mutiny from some of the religious conservatives. This could cost the republicans the president's office and pave the way for Hillary Clinton to go into the White House. James Dobson and his small group would be hurting the country if they decide not to support Rudy and break away for a possible independent run at the presidency with their candidate. We do not want to put her in the White Housevat this critical time in history.

A big discussion needs to be had by the republican party and Dobson and his group needs to smack down.

Happiness And Disappointment
10/28/2007

I have a mixture of feelings about this Louisiana election. In one respect, I am happy and in another, I am not. For the most part, I am happy because there looks to be a great deal of change coming to the legislature. I still wish the changes were even more. People like John Alario and Francis "The Fee" Thompson won. Those are two of the worst "Good Ole Boys" in this state. As bad as I think Thompson is, both he is doing it the correct way, going from the house to the senate.

If you will read Thompson's voting record, you will see just how much he has hurt the state.

Hammett "Hammered" By A Riser "ing" Star
10/29/2007

Bryant Hammett is one the worst legislators in the Louisiana. He is a person that is an Edwin W. Edwards guy. The man has made some horrible votes and is in need of, seriously, getting beat. Any person who voted for the Stelly Plan needs to go. Other than that, he has never met a tax hike that he does not like. He is one of the people that really believes, as currently constituted, a fee is not a tax. Everyone knows the opposite is true.

I can only pray that Neil Riser will win.

A Win Is A Win
10/30/2007

I do not care how it gets done, a win is win. Page Cortez beat Patrick LeBlanc in the Louisiana legislative election. LeBlanc has had some sketchy ethical questions, and in the current political environment of the state, the people will not accept this. When you have the FBI investigating you, you are in some deep manure.

The Replacement
11/01/2007

Bobby Jindal is now the Governor Elect of the state of Louisiana. This good man, whom everyone thinks will do a good job, will have to step down from his seat in the House of Representatives. We should have no problem with the person who ends up in this office because that district is a conservative republican district. There are nine candidates for that office. Who will get elected? We will see.

Now We Know
11/03/2007

When former governor Dave Treen started to come out for the release of Edwin W. Edwards, it did not pass the smell test. Why? Because he is supposed to be a republican and his nickname is "Clean". The reason he did this is to put himself in position to go after Bobby Jindal's seat in the United States House of Representatives. The problem with that is the people in the district are conservative and much more conservative than Treen. There is no shot that they would be for him and his "let out plan", as I call it. They understand what Edwin W. Edwards has done to this state. Treen is fighting a losing battle.

All They Have To Offer
11/05/2007

A great democrat, Franklin Delano Roosevelt, once said "We have nothing to fear but fear itself." He said this in the trying times of World War II. It appears that Rush Limbaugh was right when he said that the democrats have reworked the quote so that it now is twisted to state, "All we have to offer is fear itself." On the local front, what "they" have to fear is Governor Bobby Jindal. This man of color is a man of character. He truely wants to reform this state. The democrats and their willing accomplices in the press, do not want this reform to happen. They want the, seeming unstopable, gravy train of corruption to keep rolling down a hill that will take this state over a cliff, having an ultimate destination of Louisiana looking much like California.

The people on the other side of the political arena have already started to try to tear Jindal down. What they do not get, or may be they do, is Jindal does have a mandate to change this state. They tried, all throughout the election, to get him on religion. Their latest stab at this is to say, because he is a conservative republican Christian of Indian descent, he does not represent a large group of Americans of Indian descent. What they do not understand is that India is one of the fastest growing Christian nations in the world. They are assuming that most Indian Americans are democrats.

Finally, they dislike him because they know that if he can get enough legislators to think the same way he does, he can actually do what he has promised to do. That is what is in his opponents nightmares and has them waking up in a cold sweat.

Jindal To Help Republicans
11/06/2007

The recent election of Bobby Jindal as governor of Louisiana and the corresponding elections of a mostly republican and conservative democratic reform minded legislature, bodes well for the GOP in 2008. If one believes, as I do, this upcoming national election is possibly the most important one in recent history. There should be no doubt that we can not afford for Hillary Clinton and the democrats to make a clean sweep of the Presidency and Congress.

The state of Louisiana had been democrat since the end of reconstruction. The "Donkeys" have held a tight grip on power throughout this time and until the storms. Sure, there might have been a republican governor here or there but, on the whole, a majority of state offices has been held by a democrat. They were not all good for the state. Let us consider Edwin Edwards, for example. He was one of the most crooked politicians and he ran a political machine that has had its tentacles in every vice of this state for a very long time.

The point is, if Bobby Jindal can defeat this machine, anything can happen. This means that the national GOP should not get so down that it costs itself this upcoming election. They need to understand that this has been a congress that has done absolutely nothing and its approval ratings show it. Also, the presumptive nominee has some definite political and character weakness. She CAN be beat.

Katrina's Voting Record
11/08/2007

Mary Landrieu is in serious trouble. She, in my opinion, will lose her next election. How many times has she made mistakes and poor votes? Let us consider some of her votes. We can start with the fact that she signed the letter that was sent to Clear Channel (Mark May[s]) to try to shut up Rush Limbaugh. She voted against the repeal of the death (estate) tax, that flies in the face of the "American Dream". Most immigrants have the dream of coming to American to make a better life. To that point, they want to work hard, earn a money, and pass it on to their children. Why are democrats afraid of that? For the most part, this is how the Kennedy's, Rockerfellers, and other rich liberals got their money.

She has consistently hampered the American dream at every turn.

Who Will Be The Leader?
11/09/2007

For the success of Louisiana and the Governor-elect's programs, the second most important thing is the people in leadership in both houses of the legislature. This is very important because if he has reasonable people in those leadership positions, it will be much easier for him to get his agenda through. It cuts both ways, if they put unreasonable people in those position, there is more than an even shot that in the next election the brooms will come out again and the rest of the old guard will be cleared out of office. Why? Because the state voted heavily for Bobby Jindal and they want BIG changes.

The old guard better tread lightly.

Raise Them Up
11/10/2007

Charles Rangel and the democrats in congress are at it again. They want to raise taxes. In raising taxes, they are hurting the economy. As of now, the economy is roaring; but, if this tax hike or something like it were to pass, it would, at the least, slow down the economy. There is also a possibility that it would send the country into a recession.

Capital gains tax cuts would appear.

The marriage penalty will return.

All of the marginal rates would go up.

These tax hikes would definitely hurt any increase in jobs.

What Needs To Be Done
11/11/2007

We need to drill for oil. That is a fact that the environmental wakos need to understand. The China recently had to start rationing their oil supply. When will that happen here in America? Groups like the Sierra Club, Elf, Alf, and the World Wildlife Fund have hurt us with their activism. We have not put a drill into the ground or built for capacity in some time. Environmentalism is good, up to a point. That point is when it starts to hurt the ability of the country to effectively go about its business. Louisiana was a state that had an oil based economy at one time. It can be again, along with the rest of the states on the gulf coast. There is no telling how much oil has been left in the ground because of the aforementioned groups.

I am not saying that we should not try to find some alternate fuel sources. What I am saying is that while we make it more feasible to use alternate fuels, we should get every drop of oil we can find. If we do not, it will be more likely that our economy will fall.

A Terrorist Is A Terrorist
11/12/2007

The PKK in Kurdistan are nothing but a bunch of terrorists. The need to be treated as such. The problem is that the KRG (Kurdistan Regional Government) seems to be protecting them. The local government needs to get off their behinds and do their job. Their job is to crack down on this terrorists groups, especiallly this one. If they keep refusing to address this matter, then we will have to "get'r'done" for them.

Chocolate City Corruption
11/13/2007

Mayor of New Orleans, Ray Nagin, might be in trouble. A tie to William "Cold Cash" Jefferson is not a good thing for him. To survive politically, Nagin has to try to put some distance between himself and Jefferson. If he can not do that, he will go down very hard and very fast. Also, there is a congressman being investigated and he is Derick Shepherd. It now appears that congressman Shepherd has a tie to a felon who, apparently, has helped the congressman launder $140,000.

Nagin, Jefferson, and Shepherd are part and parcel of the problems that this state has faced for the last forty years. How many of our Insurance Commissioners have been put in jail? What about former governor Edwin W. Edwards and his son? Let us also include Cleo "Money Bags" Fields, Bob Odom, and the many others that owe, to some extent, their careers to Edwards.

Of course, New Orleans's current problems started with the Landrieu family. They have cast long shadows over that city for more that fifty years. "Katrina" Mary needs to go. She continues to embarrass herself, the city, and the state.

Is The Economy In Trouble?
11/14/2007

With the national trade debt rising, the worth of the dollar falling, and other forces happening, there could be a recession on the way. This recession is being predicted by a group of pessimistic democratic economists. If this recession is to happen, it would happen even quicker if one of the democrats would wind up in office. Why? Because they would raise taxes. They feel that the tax rates are too low. They long for the days right before Reagan came to power when the marginal rate was 70%. At that time, also, the death tax was in full effect. The dividend taxes and other taxes on stocks were extremely high. There was a marriage penalty. All of this and the shortages of oil led to the Jimmy Carter recession and the national misery index.

All of this has a very big possibility of happening again if one of the democrats get into office. They all want to take one third of the U.S. economy (healthcare) and put it under governmental control. They want us to be less safe and less well off. There is a difference in being poor in America and being poor in the rest of the world. Being poor in America means having an average size home. It means having at least one car. You really should not miss any meals. There is at least one television set in the residence. That is truly the case.

Clean
11/15/2007

In Denham Springs, there appears to be a clean race being wage by both men running for the district 71 legislative seat. These are to older gentlemen that, it seems, do not want to run dirty campaigns. Everyone in this state knows what dirty campaigns are. The candidates run negative adds personifying the other candidates bad qualities. These two gentlemen do not want to engage in this type of campaigning. Pope, who was on the school board, and Ware, a lobbyist, both have the experience that it take to help move this state forward. They have, both, had their dealings with good, clean politicians and crooked, dirty politicians.

Both seem to know the difference.

Even though they are older and nearing retirement they are going to be part of the new blood that will change the state for the better and move this state forward.

A Grand Dream
11/16/2007

America is the country of big dreams. The democrats have a very big dream. This dream is to win the White House, the Congress, and a plurality of governorships and legislators. The liberals hope, should Hillary Clinton get elected she will have coattails. They are hoping and praying if Rudy Giuliani is the candidate, the GOP will not unite behind him. They, also, want to run against a candidate George W. Bush would endorse.

The problem is, what will happen if the opposite happens? What if the candidate IS Giuliani and the entire republican party unites behind him?

That could be the political version of Katrina, Rita, and the western forest fires. If the republicans run a good candidate against the democratic choice, the presidential election could end up as a political tsunami. As the election nears, the democrats continue to open the proverbial door on their noses. They have tried to raise taxes, pass immigration laws, and cut off the funding for the war in Iraq. None of these have worked. If they continue, the democrats WILL be on their way to the same dominated feeling they had after the elections of 1980, 1984, and 1994. In 1980 and 1984, the democrats were whitewashed. Jimmy Carter and Walter Mondale won only one state each. Those states were their respective home states. In 1994, the GOP took back congress for the first time in forty years. That could happen again.

Will it? I don't know.

Could It? Yes it could

Meeting?
11/16/2007

There was scheduled to be a meeting of the Louisiana Airport Authority. The purpose of this meeting was to begin preliminary plans for a proposed cargo airport. The preposed site was to be in the Donaldsonville/river parish area. Why was this meeting cancelled? I believe if the members of the LAA wanted to be there, they would have made a effort. That meeting needs to be rescheduled and take place. The airport will help the Donaldsonville/Baton Rouge Area. With the jobs it would create, it would set an economic boom to the river parish area. It could, also, help the rest of the state, as this airport could be the hub of the cargo traffic in the state. It would take the cargo traffic away from the passenger airports and the passenger airports could give better service to passenger travel.

There is supposed to be a study to find the perfect position to put th airport.

They need to have the meeting, allocate the funds for the study, allocate the money, and get the airport built. They need to do this as soon as possible.

Big Boom
11/17/2007

This is a roaring economy. Every type of wealth in this great country has increased. The "poor" in America still remain to be the richest "poor" of the world. Everyone's salary has risen. Productivity is up. There is low interest rates leading to more people buying houses, cars and other things.

With all of this good stuff happening, why are democrats hollering about raising taxes?

If taxes are raised, the growth we have had will be stunted. Any other growth that could take place will not happen. In fact, raising taxes will help to bring about a recession.

The Day
11/17/2007

Today is run off day in Louisana. There are a lot of runoff elections that are very important to the success of Governor-elect Bobby Jindel. Most of the races hinge on the fact that there are a lot of former Edwin Edwards people who need to be defeated. One of the legislators who needs to go is John Alario. If he is reelected he will be a thorn in the side of Governor Jindel. We will not be suprised if some of the bad legislators get back in. Before voting the people should look at candidate's voting records to see just how bad they really are.

For the best of the state, there needs to be a lot of new people in office.

#1 Issue Of Our Time
11/18/2007

Frank Rich is right when he says the democrats are seen as wimps on national security. In this case perception is reality. They have not been strong on security since John F. Kennedy.

The question that I have is:

What would John F. Kennedy and the remaining historical hawks of the democratic party think of the current crop of democrats?

Whatever you think of how Kennedy handled the "Bay of Pigs", he stood as strong as he could in the Cuban Missile Crisis. Franklin Roosevelt and Harry S. Truman won World War II. Roosevelt recognized the great threat of evil (Naziism and Fascism) in his time. He knew this war had to be won by the side of good. Truman had the tough decision of using the atomic bomb to save American lives and the lives of the rest of the world. Truman knew if he did not use the bomb the war would drag on and on; maybe until there would have been a possibility of the evil people winning the war. Then, there was Andrew Jackson. If he had not won the battle of New Orleans there could have been a definite possibility that the British could have reneged on the treaty of Ghent and continued the War of 1812.

These democratic "Lions of National Defense" must be turning over in their graves.

Balance Beam
11/20/2007

For a long, long, time New Orleans has been a big part of the democratic "Good Ole Boy" network political machine. They had their "get out and vote" machine that would operate during any and all local, statewide, and national elections. This "machine" was concerned with the numbers of living voters, and getting them out to vote; no matter what it took. The "machine", also, sought out and found dead people and saw to it they voted. These dead people had not been taken off the voting rolls.

"Katrina" Mary Landrieu is deathly afraid of the big demographic shift of voters brought about by an act of God. The storms have caused a shift in many voters the "machine" controlled. There was a tenuous balance between the way the "machine" worked and the continuing poorness of New Orleans. They tried to allow the people that moved from the state, and set down roots in other places, the ability to vote because of the aforementioned fear. Mitch, Mary's brother, got his behind beat and beat bad, in the mayoral election. That put the fear of the Almighty in her. Then, there is the very popular state treasurer, John Kennedy. He is more likely to run against her. There is definitely a section of the city of New Orleans that will not vote for her. She is in trouble.

This could be a state that might be, solidly, in the republican's column. The people, by and large, want change.

Cut Me Mick
11/21/2007

Every sane person hates taxes. We know one thing for sure, that any of the democrats that are running for the office of the president will raise taxes to here-to-fore unseen levels. Republicans, on the other hand, are arguing with each other on who will cut taxes the most. That is an argument that, in the end, will benefit everyone in the country. Any republican in a "blue" city or state can cut taxes only so far. The people of those "blue" cities and states will allow a mayor or governor to cut those taxes because they believe in the redistribution of wealth.

I am all for the fair tax program. I really do not know if there is enough impetus to get rid of the income tax. If we can not get the fair tax, then, we should try to get a 10% flat tax. My feel is that, "If ten percent is good enough for God, then it should be good enough for the government."

Finally, I wonder if people know that for the first couple hundred years, there was no income tax in this country I have always asked the questions:

1. How did some of the major players (Rockerfellers, Kennedy's) get their monies?

2. Why don't they want everybody to live the American dream?

The American dream is to work hard, earn riches and be able to make the lives of our children and grandchildren better.

The Mayors
11/21/2007

For the most part, the mayors of Iberville Parish citieshave done a good job in their time in office. This is a time of growth in the entire parish. I will say it now, as I have said it before, the biggest impediment to unprecedented growth in this parish is the big land owners. The more of the land that they hold on to, the less this parish will grow. Back to the point of the excellent mayors, these mayors want to know how Governor Bobby Jindal and his administration will affect the improvement of their cities.

I think that when it all comes down to it, the Bobby Jindal administration will be good for Iberville.

Trust
11/21/2007

Trust is trust. Karen Gaudet-St. Germain is a democrat. We, as her constituency, really need to pay attention to how she votes on the big issues. I am not sure of whether she is a part of the "Good Ole Boy"network. The way she votes on issues like ethics reform and taxes will tell the story. If she is term limited out in 2010, then, we should thank God for term limits.

Movie Money
11/22/2007

Everyone knows how liberal most of Hollywood is. For the most part, the stars, directors, producers, and studio heads are very democrat and liberal. However, there are definite corps conservative people in that town. The problem is that these people can not come out and be conservative and get the big jobs in the big blockbuster movies. That is sad. You only need to look at Lee Majors. After the Six-Million Dollar Man and The Fall Guy, he has not gotten a whole lot of major roles because he is outwardly conservative. Sure, he has worked on a B-movie here and there, but the A-list, big budget movies have not come his way. Seeing this, the rest of the conservatives in tinsel town recoil at saying that they are conservative. That is called being black balled are black listed.

That is the way conservatives are shut down in Hollywood.

Hammett Got "Ham" Boned
11/23/2007

Bryant O. Hammett lost his election in the Louisiana legislative house. He deserved to lose. This man was one of the worst legislators in the history of the state. He was another long time office holder. He has had personal and moral problems. All one has to do is to look at Hammett's voting record. Neil Riser has no record. That was to his benefit in this election and helped to get him elected.

Riser and all of the newly elected legislators need be careful. If they do not vote the way their electorates elected want them to, they will be gone as fast as they got in.

The Pledge
11/24/2007

Mitt Romney and Mike Hackabee recently signed a no tax pledge. Why don't the rest of the top candidates take the pledge? What are they afraid of? The other candidates are afraid if they sign the no tax pledge they will have a Bush forty-one moment. They want to reserve the right to raise taxes.

There is a majority of the American people that want lower taxes or no taxes. When there are lower taxes, it has been proven over and over, the economy roars. It has, also, been proven that lower taxes bring in more revenues to the federal government.

It is not very likely that the democrats will want to lower taxes and take the pledge. They want to tax and spend. They want to redistribute wealth. That is not the American dream. The American dream is to work hard for the majority of your life, make life better for your kids, and leave the money to your children. Whereas, the democrats want to take the money and give it to people ho do not have any. They want the votes. If one has earned money fair and square, he/she should be able to do what he/she wishes with it.

Huck-A-Warming
11/25/2007

There are a lot of people, like myself, who think that the global warming controversy, as it is currently constituted, is a political hoax. Oh sure, it may very well be happening, but humanity has less to do with it then some scientists think.

The people on the Al Gore side of the argument want the government to take care of the problem. Then, there are the people like Mike Huckabee, who want the private side to take care of this problem.

We do need to work on the alternative fuels; but until that part gets figured out, there needs to be a great concentration on getting as much out of traditional fuel sources as we possibly can. Huckabee is promotine the need to accrue as much oil, natural gas, and coal as we can process. As far as the processing side, we need more refineries. We have the best chemists and chemical engineers in the world. You really are going to tell me that we can not invent a synthetic gas that could alleviate the problem?

As far as alternative fuels, we need to get it where it is feasible for the general public to use. The best alternative fuel is nuclear. If France can do it, why can't we. Solar is too expensive. Wind, in some places, just will not work because there is not enough wind to drive the turbines. The costs of both corn and sugar types of ethanol, has not been feasible to produce.

It all comes down to national security. The way the environmental wack-o's are hurting the progress of alternative fuels is by standing in the way of the businesses ability to get the oil.

Demo's Dilemma
11/26/2007

There are many dilemmas the democratic presidential candidates would put this country in if elected. If the elected president does not do something about Iran, we will have an awful mess on our hand. "President" Amadinejad and his bosses the Mullahs need to be taken care of quickly. They are threatening the world and it appears that we and the coalition of the willing will have to go take them out. They want to destroy both us and Israel.

The dilemma comes when the decision has to be made to continue the war in the middle east. That would put the administration at odds with the anti-war, far left of the democrat party.

Do they do what they were hired to do, protect the country?

Or

Do they play to their kook-fringe base?

Battling Sunnis
11/28/2007

In the period of United States history called the wild west, when there weren't enough lawmen to go around, there were vigilance committees. These were groups of people that got fed up with crime and decide to do something about it. That is what is happening with the people of Iraq. They are getting sick and tired of people coming in and stopping what appears to be the healing and rebuilding of their country. These people are starting to see the light at the end of the tunnel. The Iraqi sheik's local tribesmen are helping with the ejection of Al-Queda and other terrorist groups from Iraq.

If things keep going this way, America and her coalition will be out of there by the end of the Summer of 2008.

We will see.

Iran Should I-Run
11/30/2007

If Iran should continue in the same vain as they are going now, the fear they bring to the middle east will eventually come to the shores of America. We must not allow that to happen. It is not just the fear that our country will be attacked; it is, also, the fear that the entire middle east will go nuclear in response to Iran. As of this point, in that part of the world, there are less that a handful of countries that have nuclear (weapons). Israel, India, and Pakistan are those countries. We already are walking a tightrope with India and Pakistan in terms of trying to have them keep their nuclear "guns" in their "holsters". We understand the fear of the other countries in that region. We are allies with Israel and that make them fear Iran even more. They know if Iran gets the bomb that, other than Israel, if they should go against Iran, "President Tom" and his bosses, the Mullahs, will not hesitate in attacking them.

Iran needs to understand that the world community will not allow a country with leaders as crazy as theirs to have nuclear weapons.

New Council
12/01/2007

Because of the lower number of African Americans in the city of New Orleans, there is an all white city council. This has not happened since before th early 1980's. There are now less blacks than there are whites people in the "Big Easy". Most predicted this was going to happen sooner rather than later. It seems the democrats try to rig the election process for people who no longer live in the state to be able to vote. This did not work. This tells us that not only was the elections of Ray Nagin and " Cold Dollar" Bill Jefferson a fluke, but, it would also be a fluke if "Katrina" Mary Landrieu would win her election next year. That is why she wants to rebuild the projects in New Orleans. She actually thinks that the people who have moved away and are doing well will want to move back into that misery.

Political Murder
12/02/2007

We see shows like Hunter, Diagnosis Murder, and K-Ville that are not only police dramas but are also murder mysteries. In these shows, the murders occurs and the person who does it gets caught. There is a great murder mystery going on in the U. S. Congress. This Mystery is:

Why is a congress that was elected by such a large margin slowly impaling itself on the proverbial stake?

69

The more the democrats open the door, the more they open it on their noses and bloody themselves. It is a vicious cycle, they just can not help it, it keeps happening over and over again. Maybe they need Doctor Kavorkian to put them out of their misery. It is ugly and sad to watch a once great party that was once strong on national defense wither and die on the vine.

They have tried everything to end the war in Iraq and nothing has worked. They are now trying to find a way to cut off the funding without further angering the middle of the country who wants, for the most part, win the war. They have promised to do things that they have not come close to accomplishing. They are heading to a very big defeat, if not in this election, then in upcoming elections.

I have asked the question before:

What would the great national defense luminaries of their party (Andrew Jackson, FDR, Harry S. Truman, and JFK) think?

Not even the house will be able to save them. They will go down and they will go down hard.

The Split
12/03/2007

Even splits in state legislatures and the United States Congress are generally good things. This means that things are more than likely to get done. This also means that there is a great possibility major reforms will get passed. We will have to see what happens with ethics because there are still some very shady people in the legislature, fighting tooth and nail against change. Those types of people want the "Good Ole Boy" network gravy train to keep rolling along. That can not be allowed to happen. It will be a fight to get done what needs to be done.

I hope that some of the "new" congressmen do not allow themselves to get corrupted. and become a part of the "Good Ole Boy" network gravy train.

Secure
12/04/2007

Iraq is getting more and more secure as the days go by. Al-Queda has largely been run out of the country, and now, we are working on the Shia terrorists and insurgents that are coming in from Iran. The leaders of Al-Queda in Iraq are fighting amongst themselves. That is a very good thing. I think that even if they get their act together they will be in a much weaker position to affect Iraq. The longer they fight amongst themselves the longer the Iraqi police force and military get intrenched. As this continues to happen, the entire country gets safer and it is more likely that a political solution will be found. When a political solution IS found, we will, for the most part, be out of there. Sure, there will be an embassy and a military base there, but that is to be expected. An embassy is needed because we (The U.S.) want to keep political ties with Iraq. A military base is needed because America wants to keep a close eye on both Iran and Pakistan.

Arab Youth Yearning
12/05/2007

The Gen-X generation of the middle east hunger for freedom. Freedom is the natural state of the human spirit. This is why the president's policy of bringing freedom and democracy to the middle east is spot on correct. If this policy takes strong effect, then it will make it more likely the American interests will be able to be defended with a very small footprint.

It is said that the "Children are the future." If that is the case, and it is, then the future will be very bright. The changes in that part of the world will come fast.

Complex
12/06/2007

People, no matter what they say, are not as simple as they profess to be. Case and point is Mike Huckabee. Some people call him a rhino republican, some call him a populist, and some call him a republican. He appears to be the true social conservative. He wants to get rid of the income tax and the IRS. I would wager to say that many people would not shed a tear if both the income tax and the IRS went away. He speaks of letting the free market take care of global warming. You can believe him when he says that he will appoint "constructionist" judges.

Technically, he did raise taxes while he was a governor, but he had to deal with a state house that was very liberal and had to give up something to get something better to improve the state.

He is a complex guy who appears to have some pretty ground breaking ideas.

Marriage
12/07/2007

Recently the lame duck, New Jersey legislature, took on the controversy of Civil Unions. Civil Unions, if passed, would redefine marriage. What marriage is, and should be, is a coming together of one man and one woman. Thats what it is, has been, and should always be. The homosexuals want it to be something totally different. They want it to be between a man and a man; or a woman and a woman. That is just not right.

You have to understand this lame duck legislature is a very liberal one; and is trying to get this law passed before the next legislature, which is more conservative, comes to power.

What Is Murder
12/08/2007

In my mind murder is murder. Recently, a court ruled that when a man who shot his girlfriend; and also killed the fetus she was carrying, committed double murder. It was obvious that this man did not want the baby. He assumed his girlfriend, also, did not want the baby. We do not know the argument that ensued, that ended up in this senseless murder.

This decision by this unassuming district judge (Sharon Keller), who made the ruling, is another nail in the coffin of the current abortion law. She said "The 'compelling state interest' along with the accompanying 'viability' threashold, has no application to a status that prohibits a third party from causing that death of a woman's unborn child against her will." The supreme court smacked down the man's appeal and agreed with "Her Honor". If a woman does not want the procedure, gets killed along with her unborn baby, that means it is a double murder.

It was lucky that this case took place in a more conservative state because if it had taken place in California, the charge of murder of the fetus would not have seen the light of day.

Another Example
12/09/2007

I recently read an article about a threat of impeachment by current congressman and presidential candidate Joe Biden. The threat is "If President Bush decides to unilaterally attack Iran, I will move to impeach." He also said, "If you're going to impeach, you had better impeach Cheney first."

What does he not understand? Impeachment is a loser. Do they not see the polls that have the president's public approval on the steady incline? Do they not hear our "coalition" talk and and make threats to Iran? I do not think they do. If they would just look and listen at the world's security situation, they would not continue to make those threats.

This a another example that Joe Biden, and all his democratic friends against saving the middle east, are blind, deaf, and dumb.

Economic Panel
12/10/2007

All of the businesses of Louisiana want a better business climate. It is such a poor climate right now that small businesses open and close staying in business no less than one year. Big businesses just pack up and move away. Those types of scenarios need to be lessened and eventually reversed. If they are not, the state will continue to circle the drain and eventually go down it.

Those are the facts. If the "Good Ole Boy" network refuses to see it then whoever did not get voted out in this election will get voted out the next time.

Venezuelans For Democracy
12/11/2007

Recently, the people of Venezuela smacked down Hugo Chavez's amendments to the constitution that would have made that country a communist state. The people were right in the way they went about it. They made a big stink about it by protesting in the streets. This, in turn, received the attention of the world. It did not allow Chavez to steal the election. Until that point, he had been consolidating his power. He was cracking down on people that did not agree with him by shutting down the media. He, also, put people in jail. This "president" is the epitome of the old style communist (Castro, Lenin, Chi-Com, Kim Jong-IL) type leaders. They are all the definition of evil.

Gone Is Good
12/12/2007

Michael Olivier is, and has been, one of the goodyest of "Good Ole Boys". This person was one of the politicians that stood in the way of ethics reform. Ethics was a big deal in this last election. We, as a people, voted for ethics reform. Because Olivier opposed this bill he needed to go and he went.

Castro's Motives
12/13/2007

Recently, Fidel Castro warned Hugo Chavez about the United States trying to assassinate him (Chavez). Castro is worried about his "economy." Without the oil that comes in from Venezuela, his (Castro's) economy would be in worse shape than it is already in. He uses the oil to make himself and his party cronies rich. He, also, does not want Cuba to be the only communist state in this hemisphere.

I maintain that if both of these leaders were not in the position they are in, this would be a better world. They both oppress their people.

Castro knows that he is on his last leg and he does not want his brother to appear weak. If Ramon appears weak, that would give the United States and the Cuban ex-patriots the impetus to go for freedom and democracy.

Quality People
12/14/2007

It appears that Governor-elect Bobby Jindal is in the process of hiring quality people to serve in his administration. On December 4th it was reported that he has hired several well qualified people to be in his cabinet. All of these people have, in some way, helped to improve the state.

Recently, Ray Nagin, the Mayor of New Orleans, submitted his budget for the upcoming fiscal year. This budget included a $5 million dollar increase in taxes. This is just a democrat being a democrat. New Orleans is on the way back and he wants to increase taxes? What does he not get? If he raises taxes, it will stunt the rebuilding of the city. The New Orleans city counsel may all be democrats but they understand how lower taxes will help the city come back. The New Orleans Chamber of Commerce understands that higher taxes will not be conducive to people starting new businesses or currently operating businesses; hiring on new employees or adding to the business capital.

Fear Itself
12/16/2007

"Katrina" Mary Landrieu is deathly afraid. She is scared, and rightly so, that she has only a 50/50 shot of winning the next election. Because of hurricane Katrina, her voting base has dwindled and the machine that she used is much smaller. John, Kennedy, her opponent, has done a yeomen's job of fighting against the misuse of the peoples money as the state treasurer. This man is a well loved and a popular politician. If the demographics have definitely changed, she is going to have a tough time getting reelected.

Correcting Our Bad Reputation
12/19/2007

The bad ethics reputation by our Louisiana politicians is well founded and well deserved. There are numerous documented cases of vote buying. Politicians have allowed their families and friends to lobby them. There have, also, been many cases of laundering of money. The gravy train needs to stop.

My only question is this:

Will the change that is brought about by the election of new political leaders be enough to overcome the "Good Ole Boy" network?

Say 'No' To Big Government
12/20/2007

There are many different types of religion in America. There are the God fearing (Catholic and Protestant) ones. There is the religion of liberalism. This includes, but is not limited to, Environmentalism, Abortion, and big government.

Big government says the individual needs all the help he can get and that help comes from the government. This flies directly in the face of freedom and the free market. Freedom means that one must pull himself/herself up by the bootstraps.

In the case of the current housing 'bubble', there are some that want the government to bail out the people who took out bad home loans and the companies that made them. There were two mistakes made. One mistake was made by the lenders and the other made by the people taking out the loans. If there are investors that want to come in and buy out the companies to help eliminate the debt, then so be it. Why should we bail out people that have made the mistake of taking out loans they can not repay? That is not how democracy is suppose to works.

Backfire
12/21/2007

In Johnstown, Iowa, Mike Hackabee took an awful big risk. This risk was a criticism on how President George W. Bush is handling the middle east situation.

Huckabee wants the kind of oomph that John McCain had in 2000. He wants to be considered a maverick.

He has criticized the president on pulling away from Iran and alienating the rest of the world from the United States. That last point is totally untrue. We still have the former soviet satellites plus a few other in the coalition of the willing.

Do not get me wrong, I do like a lot of what Huckabee is saying and would probably vote for him in the general election, but he needs to moderate his stance on this one particular issue.

Why?
12/22/2007

Noble Ellington wants to be the head of the Louisiana Legislature's House Appropriations Committee. I loathe to think of that because he is a holdover from the 'bad' old days. He has been there a long time and is a Edwin W. Edwards guy. I am not saying he can not change his stripes, but it is unlikely he will.

I just do not get why Governor Bobby Jindal wants him in that position. Jindel must feel there is a debt owed to northeast Louisiana; but, the governor got votes from, elsewhere, throughout the state. I hope this is not a sign of gridlock, but a sign of foreword thinking. If Ellington gets the job, we will have to see if a leopard CAN change his stripes.

Tax Themselves Out
12/23/2007

The democrats are in trouble in their wish to raise taxes. We know that the democratic party, since the late sixties, has migrated away from John F. Kennedy on tax policy. Kennedy cut taxes and the economy grew. He was a fiscally conservative democrat. There have been too few of those types of democrats recently. For the most part, democrats are known to be "tax and spend" liberals. This is a big issue in the next election because the economy is now roaring.

Recently, the democrats have failed in raising taxes. They got smacked down when they tried to pass the Charles Shumur tax plan. A majority of the so called "blue dog" democrats have voted for tax hikes. This is the liberals opening the door on their noses again. They tried to play with names and terms. PAYGO , as it is so called, is actually a tax hike. Anything that hits Americans in the pocket book makes real Americans nervous.

Their heads are in the guillotine and the blade is about to come down on the democrats.

Coming In
12/24/2007

Immigration is a huge issue. It is a big issue all over the country. If it were not for 9/11, it would not be so; and we would be happy the with status quo. The majority of the country is afraid of what might take place if a terrorist comes across the border with a nuke, dirty bomb, chemical, or biological bomb. I am starting to believe it will take a bombing of a major city or a major land mark for the politicians to get the message. I have always asked the question:

1. What would happen if a terrorist hit the Mall of America?

Another question is:

2. Due to the numbers at sporting events, what if a terrorist hit a major sporting event?

Just Imagine if someone tried to hit the Super Bowl. It would be like the Sarajevo Olympics.

Let's hope that scenario does not happen.

Money Gulf
12/25/2007

There is a definite difference in what each party thinks about taxes. There are the tax-cutting republicans and the tax-and-spend democrats. The democrats are considered to be like Robin Hood. He robbed from the rich and gave to the poor. Robin Hood's story is more complex than that. There are marked difference between Robin Hood and the democrats. Liberals are, for the most part, secular. Robin Hood was a religious person. The democrats loathed the military. In the legion of Robin Hood, he went off and participated in the crusades, which were totally military in nature. The last thing is the libs believe in high taxes. What was the main thing that Robin Hood fought against when he came back from the crusades? It was high taxes.

When people file their taxes every year, they have to spend at lease a couple of hours fooling with the rules in trying to figure out just how much they owe.

I wonder if a great majority of the people in this great country know that for the first one hundred and twenty-six years of its existence, America did not have an income tax.

All forms of taxes are bad . They are bad because they penalize achievement.

The American dream is to make enough money, to make the lives of our children better. The death/inheritance tax penalizes the dead and the living. The dead have already paid taxes on that money. Why should their kids have to pay on the money again? I would like to point out how hypocritical the libs are on this issue. Senator Ted Kennedy and Senator/Representative Jay (Exxon/Standard Oil) Rockafeller, for the most part, got their money though inheriting it. That is the American way. Why would they not want the great majority of the country to have that ability as well?

How Many More
12/26/2007

We have several insurance commissioners in jail. It all goes back to ethics. When you try to create something that appears to be good, but end up being bad, that is a problem. We have three insurance commissioners in jail and there is a possibility that there could be a fourth. That is why ethics reform was such a big issue in the last election.

These office holders committed crimes like extortion, mail fraud, false statements, and now the latest is price fixing. Those are some serious crimes and they definitely needed to be punished.

Right Turn
12/27/2007

It seems some of our friends in the coalition of the willing are going conservative. Look, for instance, at France, Germany, and now South Korea. The geopolitical ramifications of this happening are yet to be seen. South Korea got tired of having liberal presidents, that did very little. They, also, seem to want a tougher stance on North Korea. The people of South Korea have also voted for a stronger relationship with the United States. It seems that inflation had taken affect and their was not enough economic growth. When all of this happens, the party in charge usually gets booted out.

No FEC
12/28/2007

The Federal Elections Commission is the entity that makes sure that elections are fair and equitable. The democrats are blocking a presidentual nominee to the FEC. This blocking is being done because the nominee is a republican. The idiot, Harry Reid, will not allow the president's nominee to go through. This is another in a long line of Faux Pas the democratic leadership has made. This , much like everything else the lowest ranked congress in the history of the country is doing, will blow up in the democrats face. If this continues, there will be no FEC.

Bye, Bye, Mr. Go
12/29/2007

It now appears that the Mississippi River Gulf Outlet will be out of here. It is generally felt that MRGO has been a major reason that the Louisiana wetlands have been eroding. By doing away with MRGO, it will better help protect Louisiana during major and minor hurricanes.

Some People
12/30/2007

Some people fear what they do not understand. Mike Huckabee would be good for the nation. His opponents think he represents "compassionate conservatism" on steroids. He may want a nanny state, and that is bad. The main thing that he is in favor of is eliminating the IRS. That would definitely be a good thing.

Children Are The Future
01/01/2008

When Benazir Bhutto was assassinated recently, it was her dream of democracy for Pakistan died with her. The Pakistan People's Party (PPP) needed a new head. Children are and will be the future because her nineteen year old son Bilawal was named the heir apparent. This young man, who has yet to complete his studies, will not become the Prime Minister yet. He will be is the top leader in the Pakistani Parliament. He may be the only choice to take over for his mother because some of family members (aunts) do not want the honor and pressure that goes along with the duties. There is, also, other choices that have legal matters that are pending against them and would be more controversial choices to succeed Benazir Bhutto.

In my opinion, the election that was slated to take place on January 8, has to occur to keep the country together. If it (the election) does not, then not only does this country slip into civil war, but it will also have a chance to be taken over by Al-Quieda. That is THE nightmare situation. If this situation happens, not only does Al-Quieda get the country it needs but is also gets the nuclear material that it needs too.

What Is Privacy?
01/02/2008

The attacks on the World Trade Center changed a lot of things, not only here, but in the rest of the world. The privacy advocates can thank the terrorists for the west cracking down on privacy rights. If not for the terrorists, maybe a lot of the governmental laws passing would not have happened in as short a time. Terrorists are dumb in this respect, if they had not attacked, America and the rest of the world would not be doing such things as freezing their cash flow. These crack downs have made it difficult for the terrorists to conduct operations. Also, what has happened is that most countries have turn against the terrorists and they are finding no respectable country wanting to harbor them; for fear the rest of the world will shun them.

What Is Happiness?
01/03/2008

Happiness, in general, means different things to different groups of people. The Iraqi citizenry, in specific, the Iraqi youth, are very happy. The reason for this happiness is Saddam Hussein is gone and the threat of terror against them has radically dropped. The young in Iraq have thirsted for freedom for a long time.

That is why it was good for America to attack Iraq.

Roll Of The Dice
01/04/2008

Pinnacle Corporation wants to build another casino in Baton Rouge. The success of a new casino should not be questioned. There will always be people who like to gamble. The problems start with the up tick in crime that will accompany another casino. The other thing that will happen is more gamblers and the treatment for the addiction to gambling.

Sure, it will lead to a better economy, because of the favet there will be some hiring of new workers; but at what cost?

Good and Bad
01/05/2008

Most politicians have good and bad qualities about them. Ron Paul and Mike Huckabee are no different. Huckabee is a populist republican while Paul is a dove. Both may be rhinos (republican in name only), but they are getting a lot of play. Paul has raised a lot of money, while Huckabee has cause a stir with some of his policy ideas. Can either of these people win? I don't know. Do they have a shot? Yes. With the fact that none (McCain, Giuliani, and Romney) of the frontrunners have pulled away, means any of these candidates have a shot to win the nomination.

What Is Public Opinion
01/06/2008

Opinions are like behinds, everybody has one. According to surveys, "green" cars are not wanted by a majority of a plurality of the American people. The government is trying to force higher fuel efficiency standards. Again, a majority and a plurality of the American people do not want higher fuel efficiency standards. The people like things as they are.. The only ones who want this to happen are the Washington, inside-the-beltway, elites. Theses people just don't get it.

Comeback
01/07/2008

Slowly but surely, the city of New Orleans is coming back from the worst combination disaster in the history of our country. The rebuilding process is long and will remain slow. There will be another infusion of money coming in a few months and the Corps of Engineers can get to work correcting the dual problems of the Mississippi River Gulf Outlet and the rebuilding of the levees. These two projects are needed to protect this great American city.

In terms of the people returning, the ones wanting to come back will and the ones that are happy where they are, will stay where they are currently located. The ones that do come back are the ones that want to actively participate in the cities recovery.

Help To The Platform
01/08/2008

We really do not know how much help Governor-elect Jindal will receive from the legislature. The numbers of votes he got in the election do not appear to be as great as they were once thought to be. Yes, the republicans won the Speaker of the House, but the amount of the vote numbers arc razor thin. It may be harder than thought to pass his agenda. Jindal not only has to deal with the democrats, but he also will have to deal with some rhino republicans. Some of the those politicians say they have changed, but their history is that they have been in the back pocket of the "Good Ole Boy" network. I am not going to waste space here on their names. What I will say is that the governor-elect needs to know who they are, because the general populace sure knows. These are the people who have been running this state into the ground for the last forty or so years.

These people should have been gone a long time ago.

Can He Win?
01/09/2008

Mike Hackabee is running for the office of President of the United States. Can he win? Will he win? The answers to those questions are, "we don't know." It can not be argued that Huckabee is a likeable guy. He also has a charisma that can not be denied. He has the ability to make fun of himself and take serious hits and come back from it. There are definite holes in his platform. Will he be able to overcome his shortcomings? He will have the ability in the more liberal states; but, when it comes to the deep south, I am not so sure. Just take a look at the state of Louisiana. Louisiana WILL go republican and the republicans in this state are fairly conservative. Huckabee, on the other hand, seems not to be. The point is, he may very well be the nominee.

Idiot American Al Qaeda
01/10/2008

Adam Godahn who is the self proclaimed leader of Al Qaeda in America, has made threats against President Bush. This man is an idiot because he thinks that the people "in the know" are not concerned about him. The fact is, as of right now, he is not at the top of the concerned list. He is not even in the top fifty. As of this point in time, this man is just a fly on the windshield of the United States. He should get it through his thick skull that we could off him, just like that. If he is all that powerful, he would be orchestrating attacks and claiming them.

Economically Up
01/11/2008

It appears that the Louisiana's economy is looking up. According to an article in the Trinton Falls, New Jersey newspaper, Louisiana is third in the nation in regards to economic development. If a state has had economic expansion and relocations it got cited in this positive report.

With this good news, it means we are, slowly but surely, turning a corner. To keep making this slow turn, the Louisiana State Government must keep doing things that will carry the state farther into the right direction. One thing that should happen is to get rid of the state income tax and to lower of get rid of taxes on businesses.

We must pay attention to what the ;egislature is doing because I think that th Governor-elect wants to do as much as he can to benefit the people.

Democrat Stimulus Package
01/12/2008

There are two different ideas for a stimulus package for the country. One talks about tax cuts to get businesses to hire new people; and to get the people to invest more in the stock market and in bonds. The other is to tax the country to the hilt. What this does is takes away the incentive for the general public to go to work. Why work, when you can get it for free? It also takes away the incentive for the business owners to hire the skilled workers; and, it also dissuades those same business owners from making a capital investments in their business.

Both Hillary Clinton and Barak Obama believe in high taxes. They, much like most other democrats, believe they are the "Robin Hoods" of America. However, they have twisted the legend. The most important part of the legend is the part that says what the legendary character did, he did because of high taxes. Yes, he stole from the rich and gave to the poor, but what he was actually doing was giving the people back their stolen tax money.

Clinton and Obama want to raise all of the marginal rates. They also want to reinstate the death tax. In short, they want to take more of your money back to Washington D.C. They think they are better suited in deciding what to do with your money.

Earthquake
01/12/2008

The power base of the state of Louisiana (brain power, money, talent) have, for the most part, come from everywhere but Baton Rouge. The most glaring example is the vast majority of the money, rightly, wrongly, lawfully, or corruptly, that has flowed to New Orleans. Sure, there was some money that went to north, west, and south Louisiana but for the most part, New Orleans was like a roach motel.

Now, with the chance that the intangibles will be spread more evenly between people from all areas of the state, maybe, we can correct some of the problems that have plagued the state for last forty years.

What has happened will be good; not only for the state, but also for the area of south central Louisiana. The "network" is shaking like they were in a California building during an earthquake.

Along with the Governor-elect Bobby Jindel, the ethics reform movement started in big, bad, Baton Rouge. A number of the Governor-elect's transition team members are from the Baton Rouge area. These people have elected some new representatives (Steve Carter, Franklin Foil, and Eric Ponti) who are supposed to give the Governor-elect a greater ability to get his agenda passed through the state legislature.

As said by Mark Ballard in his article 'BR Roots A Rarity For Governors,' "With this much power located in one place, look for more thought and creative change to come from the class of 2008."

Bipartisanship
01/14/2008

There are some people that may want bipartisanship in the congress. As of now, it is not going to happen. Look at who is in congress and who those people listen to; then, you will see just how bad it is. On the left, you have Pelosi, Reid, MoveOn.org, and Daily Kos; and on the right you have the NRA, Talk Radio, and Duncan Hunter. My point is that I think that American's want partisanship, for this is how things get done. By hook or by crook, some of the greatest legislature passed for the betterment of our nation came out of partisanship.

The Internet: The Free-est Place On Earth
01/15/2008

The Internet, much like people, has good things and bad things about it. Yes, there are sexual deviants and pedophiles there, but on the whole, there is more good on the net than bad. People like Andrew Keen, a reporter for the New York Times, are pessimists. These people look for the negative in everything. I understand the internet is a threat to his line of work; but so is talk radio. After all, he is in the mainstream/drive-by media. For the most part, he and his listening audiance, dislike the ability of the internet to be able to check and recheck their information for truthfulness. They want their narrative to be the only one. For a long time, these people have gotten away with a lot of misinformation, and have not been called on the carpet for it.

Open
01/16/2008

The Republican nomination for the office of the President of the United States is, very much, a wide open affair. One state goes for one nominee, a second state goes for another, and a third state goes, for yet, a third nominee. Who will be the nominee? We will not know until the convention. The nominee may not even be one of the persons currently running. All of the top candidates have flaws. Some are too liberal, some are too old, and others are just too boring. My hope is that someone in this crew is good enough to beat whomever the democrats puts up as their candidate.

Old Is New.
01/17/2008

After the recent Louisiana legislative election, there were lawmakers who went from one chamber of the legislature to the other. Mike Walsworth and Francis Thompson were two such lawmakers. Walsworth seems to be a good honest fellow, while Thompson has a long record of being less than ethical. Thompson says that he has turned over a new leaf, we will have to wait and see.

Governor Bobby Jindal wants to, seriously, overhaul the ethics laws of this state. I am pretty sure that Walsworth is agreeable; but Thompson, that could be another story.

Holding On
01/18/2008

It seems that what Noble Ellington did, in going to court to get a restraining order, to protect his wife's job was the ultimate in the "Good Ole Boy" network in trying to hold on to power. He went and found a corrupt judge, Don Johnson, and got him to rule in his favor. This ruling will probably not stand up because it will be appealed in the Louisiana State Court of Appeals, and ultimately, in the Louisiana State Supreme Court. Ellington had to know that with the current election results, what he was doing with his wife's job would be seriously looked at by the ethics committee. If he thinks that he will be able to get away with it, he is dumb as a stump.

Oily Wrongs
01/19/2008

The doom-sters and nay-sayers have said for a long time that oil production will peak and soon go down. I think that if we decide to go and get it, there is more then enough oil for everyone. The problem is the environmentalist "whack-o's". They refuse to let the country drill in areas that are obviously laden with oil. I do not think these "whach-o's" understand this oil is tied directly to national security. Without this oil, we will have to continue to depend on foreign oil.

What needs to happen is for the next president to tell the environmentalist "whack-o's" to take a flying leap. The problem is that these people are a major constituency to the democratic party. There are also some republicans (rhinos) who believe in the global warming hoax. These people will not do what is, obviously, necessary to get us off of foreign oil.

Are The Clinton's Racist?
01/20/2008

We are now seeing the Clinton's true face in this election. They are continually getting dirtier and dirtier, as evident by them using the "down and dirty deck of cards". They have alleged that Barack Obama is a drug head. Obama, much like some people coming of age, may have experience the drug culture. People who live in glass houses should not throw stones when they asked the question, "Can a black man be President?" How can that be construed as nothing but racism? The history of the democratic party on race is not good.

These are points in question:

-throughout the late nineteenth and early twentieth centuries, the party that continually stood in the way of civil rights reform, were democrats.

-for the most part, people that were in the KKK were in the democratic party.

-one of the leaders of the democratic party was once a Grand Wizard for the KKK.

Obama should really look out, as the race gets tighter, the dirtier the Clinton's get.

Sakozy Gets Religious
01/21/2008

Nicolas Sarkozy is not a practicing catholic but believes in the cultural aspects of the Catholic Church.

By professing his beliefs it has brought him in direct conflict with the secular progressive, socialist opposition in France. These people say by his actions he is going against the French constitutional separation of church and state. I do not agree. When a person cannot, outwardly, say he is religious, then the constitution is not worth the paper it is written on. This is another example of how religion is hated by the atheists and Christianity is hated by the secular progressives.

He believes in the hope most religions espouse and in the ability of most followers to espouse it.

More Money
01/22/2008

The Louisiana Ethics Board is woefully understaffed. They are very much like most other governmental agencies who would like to their jobs and do them well. Not having enough field workers to investigate political crimes has allowed the "Good Ole Boy" network to flourish. It is like the Louisiana High School Athletic Association with high school "recruiting". There is just not enough money or manpower to investigate all of the infractions committed.

Governor Bobby Jindal has said that ethics is high on his "to-do" list. This should include getting the money necessary for the Ethics Board to do a better job. If they are to do its job correctly, judges like corrupt Don Johnson would not be sitting on cases for his friends, namely Bob Odom. Another way in which they could do their jobs more effectively is to watch over certain elections where certain politicians are known to have stuffed the ballot box. Also, the fiascos of Bob Odom, William "Cold Cash" Jefferson, and others like would not see the light of day.

The people at the Ethics Board, no matter how good they are at their jobs, can not do the job without more backing and funding.

Where's Our Free Money
01/23/2008

The way the social security situation, now works, is that the younger generation works for the money that is given to their retired parents. The problem is that the numbers of younger workers are decreasing. There are a some reasons for this:

1. Abortion-Since Roe v Wade there has been over four million abortions a year. This means that the numbers of younger workers are decreasing and there are not a great deal of replacements workers. After WWII, soldiers came back from their duty and began procreating. The averaged family had more that 2.5 children in it.

2. Birthrates-Simply stated, there are less babies born.

3. Divorce-Everyone knows at least one person who has been divorced. Fifty percent of all marriages end in divorce.

Social security is the third rail. Any lawmaker that has touched it has died politically. The problem is that it needs to be touched over and over again; to get it fixed correctly. I am not sure that any of this current group of politicians have the guts to take it on in a straight forward fashion.

What I fear the most it that our children will never see social security.

What Is In A Lifetime?
01/24/2008

When a politician has served a long time in a particular office it is said he has experience and that experience brings about clout. But if a politician has not done anything while in office, then what kind of clout does he have? People like Richard Baker (R-Louisiana) has done some good in office. But on the whole, the great majority of the congressmen and legislators, when elected, just go along to get along. They do not propose any bills or amendments. Some seldom vote on issues.

It will be very hard for a democrat to win in Richard Baker's district. The reason, because it is a conservative district. One can not fault him for going into private business for that is where the money is.

The election replacing Richard Baker will definitely be a fun election to watch.

I would like to offer to Richard Baker "the best of luck".

Lady Leader
01/25/2008

Where are the women candidates for president? Frankly, there are not many ladies that are that talented, ambitious, or calculating. It has been speculated that at some point Codoleeza Rice may have thoughts of an elected political carrere. If she does run for office, she needs to have significant policy ideas to have an excellent shot at being elected. There are several problems with Mrs. Clinton:

1. She is not a very likable person. She comes off as cold and mean.

2. She comes off as scheming.

3. The Clinton Peccadillos.

4. Bill Clinton, her husband.

Bill just does not seem to want her to get elected. Why does he keep doing and saying things that are directly opposed to her political psylosophy?

Those are just a few reasons that she may not be elected.

Film Mistakes
01/26/2008

The people in Hollywood just don't get it. There are certain films that, when they are made, are doomed not to do well in the majority of the country; yet the film makers continue to make them. They are the same films that are usually nominated for the major awards and do not do well at the box office.

It is death to make an anti-military/anti-war film and hope it does well in the middle of the country; and in the south. Those two country areas of people are usually pro military. The political movies that do well are usually the ones with a modicum of truth about them. Great examples are "Wag The Dog", and "Primary Colors". These producers need to understand, for the most part, a good religious base movie will do well. Heroic movies like the "Die Hard" series, the "Rambo" series, "Commando", and others will always do well because the main characters all tend to end up being heros. Sports movies do extremely well because they show winners, losers, and characters that people can pull for. Science fiction speaks for itself and, basically, have a niche audience. Comedies, as long as they stay away from sending a political message, will do extremely well. Most of the political message movies are dramas. Hollywood does not get that the only preaching that mid-westerners and southerners like to hear is the preaching that occurs in church.

Will they ever get it? They won't until the youngsters in Hollywood quit buying into the ideals of the older actors, directors, and producers that represent the liberal vanguard of Hollywood; coming from the age of the sixties.

Stop The Spending
01/27/2008

America could learn a lot from French Prime Minister Nicolas Sarkozy. He has decided to place a freeze on state spending. France is one of the European socialist-like countries that is having spending problems. They have, way too many, socialist program that are, just, too taxing on the French economy.

Nicolas Sarkozy is a smart man. He knows that in the case of a state running a deficit, what has to be done is to cut spending.

The problem, for America, is that both sides of the isle just don't want to get it through their thick sculls. They want to spend on things (bridges to nowhere) that we do not need. Our national budget is just too overblown. If we could make some cuts, we would find the money to do more important other things. We could, also, continue the needed processes already going on.

Sometimes there are fights that happen that, probably, should not happen. For instance, the fight the congress will have to concern itself, again, over military spending The democrats say that they want us to find Osama Bin Laden. The problem is that it is like pulling teeth to get the money to do so. Other problem are the so called earmarks. These are programs specifically designed to get people re-elected. The king of such projects is West Virginia senator Robert "KKK" Byrd. This man has so many highways and state buildings named after him, he needs a staff to keep up with them.

Don't even speak of some of the social programs that should be overhauled or flat cut out. It is said that social security is the third rail. The program needs to be corrected fast, or else, some of the younger Americans will never be able to avail themselves of the program. There are ways to correct it but, again, the democrats stand in the way.

It seems to me that there are marked differences in the candidates that are running for president from the two parties. One side is talking about cutting spending, the other is not. The democrats want to spend us into oblivion. They want universal healthcare that would cost the country hundreds of billions of dollars. To make up for the money shortfall, they propose, guess what, TAXES. They would like to see the government take more than fifty percent of your money. Some of the republicans are just as bad, because they are not who they say they are. These people are liberal or 'rhino' republicans.

We are in a great need for a big change. The question is Will we get it?

Good Cop, Bad Cop
01/28/2008

The Clinton's are doing whatever it takes to get her elected. Bill is going out on the stump and turning on his acting chops and charisma. While doing this, he is playing the angry man. This is definitely a ploy to get Hillary's favorable ratings up. Almost fifty percent of the county hates her. That is bad because she needs fifty-one percent of the votes to win the election. People think she is a cold, calculating, stiff, humorless person. Most presidents have some redeeming qualities about them. She does not seem to have any. Every time she cackles, it hurts her.

It just seems she is nowhere near as good as her husband at selling manure and making people wanting to buy it.

Victory?
01/29/2008

Frank Rich, a reporter for the New York Times, has put forth a theory. His theory is that John McCain would be the best suited republican candidate to defeat Hillary Clinton. He says that the vetting of Mrs. Clinton has not really happen, because there are several million Bill Clinton presidential documents that have yet to be released.

That man is right

She claims experience, but where is it? The only experience she has it that of a denier and a liar. She can push things aside and under the rug. She refuses to release the documents that relate to her trying to get national health care. Why would she not release them? The reason might be because she is afraid of them, not only showing she failed, but, also showing the specifics of her idea.

She will get hammered when she decides to claim her ability is there for her to be commander-in-chief . McCain, for all of his maverick-ness, is a genuine war hero. When he speaks of national defense people listen. The man, after all, was a POW at the Hanoi Hilton.

Don't even talk about the vast right wing conspiracy. McCain is and has been a rhino. The press absolutely loves him.

It all comes down to genuine-ness. He is, she isn't. That is why there could be a sure defeat for Mrs. Clinton.

Mary, Mary, Why Ya Buggin'
01/30/2008

I don't know the exact title of this song, but there is a line in it that poses the question:

"Mary, Mary, Why Ya' Buggin"?

That is an excellent question for "Katrina" Mary Landreiu. The answer is that she fears she may lose her next election. That is a legitimate fear. She has made some poor votes on some key issues in congress. She has been a "yes" girl for the democratic party. Her voter base in New Orleans has been eroded enough that she will probably lose. She will not get help from the current mayor of New Orleans, Ray Nagin. Nagin hates the Landreiu's. Her brother Mitch got a jolly stomping in the last mayoral election because he could not get the white vote.

She needs to go and she will go.

Dragging
01/31/2008

The Army Corps of Engineers is acting like a true governmental entity. They are using their bureaucrats to slow down and impede the progress of rebuilding the Mississippi/Louisiana gulf coast. It is being said that there has to be a study done and that study is to take five years to complete. I don't buy that. It seems this process is a giant waste of the people's money.

There has to be a better, more streamlined method of doing this.

The government will always be the government. They will always look for the slowest and most costly way of completing a project.

Faulty Thinking
02/02/2008

There are some people thinking there could be an Barak Obama/Hillary Clinton ticket for the democrats. I don't go along with this thinking because of the way the democratic primary is working itself out. Those two candidate are destroying each other. With the rancor and hatred that is going on, I do not see Obama accepting her as his vice president running mate. Obama may want a more passive running mate, one he can control and one who will give him, "yes sir", lip service. Hilliary is too power hungry and wants it all.

IRS Smackdown
02/04/08

High taxes are bad.

Usually, it is not a good idea to fight the government on this issue because the government wins big. Wesley Snipes did and won. He said, "The IRS has no right, due to its own code, to collect taxes on income earned in this country." He continued, "It is not a proper government entity."

The ruling for the trial maded no sense. It exonerated him from the same felonies the government got Al Capone on. Snipes got convicted on a lesser charges, that of not filling out tax returns. Why should he have to file if he does not have to pay?

McCain Is A Four Year Death
02/05/2008

If John McCain is elected it will be just like electing a democrat. This man is as liberal, as all get out. He has made deals with people like Ted Kennedy, Russ Finegold, and Joe Lieberman. Other than the war, he has not acted like a conservative. The bill with Finegold was, so called, campaign finance reform. It opened the door for the 501-c4's like MoveOn.org. He believes in the global warming hoax. The man was in the, so called, gang of fourteen. This was a group of congressmen looking to stop the "nuclear option"; in terms of getting strict constructionist judges to the supreme court.

It will not be good for the republican party if he gets elected, for he is a rhino. He definitely has to "show me" he has changed his stripes.

Sad, Sad, Day
02/06/2008

John McCain appears to have won, yesterday, on super Tuesday. This may well drag the republican party to the center. This will not be a long term answer to the successful winning of the election by the GOP. As much as he will try to make himself over into a conservative, his senatorial record says differently.

There is not much difference between McCain and Hillary Clinton or BarakObama. Other than fighting for the surge in Iraq, his record says he is a liberal. Democrats don't like the word. Immigration is an issue that he just does not get. He wants a comprehensive immigration plan that has no consequences for people that come across the border and are illegal. What will happen if he is elected president and comprehensive immigration reform passed, will be a nightmare situation across the southern borders.

Let us now talk about campaign finance reform. This was an assault on the first amendment. Will he have the guts to correct his own bill? He also believes in the global warming hoax.

I am not sure that I can vote for McCain. I know that I can not vote for either Clinton or Obama.

Rolling Fix
02/07/2008

We all know that the roads in Louisiana need serious work. There are so many places in the state needing road repair it is tough to find a place to start. There are roads that need to be fixed all over the state. Let us start with I-55 and I-12. I-12 needs to be widened and I-55 needs to be resurfaced. Resurfacing I-55 makes all the sense in the world. The fact of the matter is, when the roads from Texas, Mississippi, and Arkansas run into the Louisiana roads at the borders, the quality goes down. This fact can not be argued.

As for the widening of I-12, it really needs to happen. It is amazing to find places in this state where the interstate narrows to a two lane highway. This makes no sense. With the way semi's use the interstate, we need to have, at least, six lanes all over the state.

Aren't We Special
02/08/2008

The governor has called a special session to try to deal with Louisiana's political ethics situation. For the last forty years the ethics of our politicians have taken a nose dive. This phenomenon began, in earnest, with Edwin W. Edwards and has not stopped since. How many insurance commissioners are in jail or in trouble? We have politicians, like Edwards and his son, currently serving jail terms. We, also, have a number of lawmakers currently under indictment like, William "Cold Cash" Jefferson. Then, there are the politicians who have gotten away with breaking the law. People like Bob Odom and Cleo "Bag of Cash" Fields, are to be mentioned. No way can we name the city and parish officials that have been tainted.

Our recently elected governor, Bobby Jindal, has promised to start us on the long and winding road to ethics reform. This will definitely be a fight because of the "Good Ole Boy" network. These are the lawmakers that have remained in power for thirty years or more and, basically, have stolen their money from the government.

These are the politicians who spend the people's money on frivolous things. They allow themselves to go down dark roads and end up in questionable positions. There are people like Noble Ellington, who is currently hiring his wife as an aide to him in the senate, while the law states he should not be able to do this.

Then, there is the term limits law that has holes in it big enough to drive a Mack truck through. These politicians meant it to be this way so they could remain elected. That is not what the people had in mind.

That is just a few reasons we need to correct our ethics problems.

☐*Burial*
02/09/2008

The mainstream press tends to bury stories that do not fit a particular template. The hindsight argument against attacking Iraq was that there were no weapons of mass destruction. A certain FBI agent was one of the agents that debriefed Saddam Hussein had said that, not only did Hussein have the programs but he wanted to continue to work towards getting bigger, better, and more destructive WMD programs. The Iraqi WMD program remained a threat as long as Saddam remained in power.

The scariest thing is when Saddam Hussein wasasked about using chemical weapons against the Kurds, he said it was "Necessary." How evil is that?

Woody's Pledge
02/10/2008

Woody Jenkins has singed a no-tax pledge. This pledge states that he will be a person who will not vote any hike in the marginal tax rate. He could be running against Mary Landrieu. She is your classic tax and spend democrat. If she should SOMEHOW get reelected, there is, almost a 100% chance she would vote for a hike in those aforementioned tax rates. We, as Louisianians, can not allow this to happen. As bad as some think the economy would be, it could be worse with the increase in taxes. Low taxes is one of the best things for the economy.

Why are low taxes the best thing for the economy?

There are many reasons. Some are:

1. It gives businesses the incentive to hire new workers.

2. It gives businesses the incentive to invest more in the companies they own.

3. Because of the extra amount of workers that are hired, there are more people who are paying taxes.

4. It gives people the incentive to go into business for themselves.

5. It also brings more revenue to the government because there are more people paying taxes.

We just can't afford for a majority of democrats to get into the house of representatives. The house is where tax laws orginate.

Importance
02/11/2008

(All information comes from the Baton Rouge Morning Advocate)

In my mind, the most important government business that should be done when Governor Bobby Jindal's administration takes office is ethics. From 1969, starting with Attorney General Jack Gremillion to today, with William "Cold Cash" Jefferson, the state of Louisiana has had an ethics problem. Jefferson is just the latest person that is in serious trouble.

Here is a list of Louisiana's less that ethical politicians since 1969.

1. Louisiana Attorney General Jack Gremillion is charged with fraud. He was also indicted for perjury. (1969)

2. U.S. Rep. Richard Tonry resigns to fight charges of obstruction, receiving illegal campaign contributions. (1977)

3. Governor Edwin W. Edwards was accused of conspiracy in trying to profit in it the approval of hospital and nursing home projects. There was a mistrial and he was later acquitted. (1985-1986)

4. Legislators passed a bill that would ease ethics code restrictions for the acceptance of food, lodging, and transportation and the acceptance of honoraria when making speeches. (1989)

5. Doug Green, who was the Insurance Commissioner, was indicted on 16 counts of wire fraud, money laundering, conspiracy, theft, and bribery in connection to the collapse of Louisiana's third largest auto insurance company. He was found guilty on all charges except theft. (1990)

6. Former four-term Insurance Commissioner Sherman Bernard pleads guilty to extortion. (1992)

7. Election's Commissioner Jerry Fowler was indicted for getting kickbacks on a scheme that involved voting machines. (1998)

8. Insurance Commissioner Jim Brown was convicted of perjury for trying to help a failed insurance company to come to a favorable settlement with the state, who was to get money from the company to pay creditors and policy holders. (1999)

9. Agricultural Commissioner Bob Odom is indicted on 21 charges of bribery, extortion, and theft. Most are thrown out, but prosecutors are now appealing to have them reinstated. (2002)

10. New Orleans City Councilman Oliver Thomas pleads guilty in taking $15,000 in bribes from a businessman to keep a city contract. (2007)

11. U.S. Rep William Jefferson is going to face trial for 16 counts of corruption for the finding of $90,000 in his freezer in a raid by the FBI. (2005)

In my mind there is one uncharged crime. This is the crime that was perpetrated on Tom Benson when he was trying to get a lease to bring a hockey team to New Orleans. Benson thought he had a deal with, then, Governor Mike Foster. Foster, at the eleventh hour, reopened the deal and ended up handing the deal to another group, which included a good friend of the governor. People at the time disliked Benson for the way he was negotiating with the state; that he did not want to think deeply about the deal.

Uncommitted
02/12/2008

I understand the tepid response to Mike Huckabee. The problem with that, is on the republican side, John McCain is not well liked. Both of these two candidates may or may not be liberals. I tend to believe that Huckabee would be more conservative than McCain. McCain has worked on such bills as campaign finance reform, comprehensive (amnesty) immigration reform, and others.

McCain is finding it hard to win over the conservatives. He seems to be going at it in a reverse fashion. He runs to the center of the party in the primary and to the right in the general election

Huckabee has made no pretensions, he has been making sure he is ties to the conservatives. He started out by getting the evangelicals in Iowa. He then took the southern states. His most important policy is he wants to get rid of the income tax in favor or a consumption or national sales tax.

Louisiana voters does not know what to make of either candidate. That is why the state remains uncommitted.

All At Once
02/13/2008

It seems they are trying to correct the ethics problems of this state in one fell swoop. Usually, when you try to do things in that manner, it does not work. Politicians take the tact of doing things in increments. This means they go piece by piece. Are they trying to get greedy? It's a possibility. Will this work? I am not sure.

I know one thing, there is going to be a huge fight from the "Good Ole Boys". These politicians want to keep this state mired in the past. They want the status quo. It is going to be a tough fight, but it will be a worthwhile battle. It will be a good first step in us trying to correct the perception this is a corrupt state and there is no one who wants to fix the problem.

Hinged Or Unhinged
02/14/2009

It seems Hillary Clinton's bid for the Presidency of the United States is slowly, but surly, coming apart. Every firewall that has supposedly been set up by the Clinton campaign has come and gone. Barak Obama won the Iowa Caucus. He won in New Hampshire. She said that Florida was her first firewall. She lost the "Sunshine State". Then came the northeast. California was her next firewall and that fell through. She had no shot in the south. The only southern state she won was Arkansas. She could not even beat Obama in New York. Her latest loss was the "Potomac" primary.

It now looks like Barak Obama is the presumptive nominee. Hillary's campaign to become the first woman president of the United States is fizzling. We are now seeing the desperation in the inner reaches of the Clinton campaign. Some of her people have already drunk the Kool-Aid. It is appears the men in the white coats are coming, fast.

What will we see when she steps aside?

Might we see a Clinton divorce?

I don't know. We will see.

Spy Lapse
02/15/2008

The democrats are about to let the Central Intelligence Agency's wire tapping program lapse. This program allows the CIA to monitor calls between Al-Queda and their friends in other countries. It allows us to, more easily, fight the war on terror.

What the democrats are doing is unconscionable. They are playing politics with national security. They do this because they hate the fact that President George W.Bush was right in going into Iraq. They also do it because they are trying to get us out of Iraq as fast as possible. The fact is, the democrats just don't want to win.

They are only following the leadership of their presidential hopefuls.

They are galactically blind.

There is success in Iraq. The surge is doing its job. It is allowing Sunni's and Shiite's to be able to reconcile.

We need this program to stay intact and active.

Leaders And Followers
02/16/2008

There are politicians of many stripes. There are crooks and liars. There are some with good character and others with bad character. There are competent and incompetent ones. Whatever kind a state gets, they hope to have a leader and not a follower.

Sometimes the people elect a person they think is a leader, but ends up having to be led around by the nose by the people.

I like Bobby Jindal. I voted for him. In the case of the Stelley Bill, the people had to lead him around by the nose. We can also say the same thing about the majority of the legislators. These people were elected to help lead the state out of the doldrums and into a new day. When our leaders did not get out in front of the issues they seemed to want to keep the status quo. For whatever reason, they just did not seem to want to get rid of the bad bills. The people wanted the Stelley Bill gone and now it is gone.

All of these new lawmakers who got into office by promising to change things are the ones the people will support. And when the lawmakers do not want to do the right thing, the people will lead them around; or lead them out of office with their votes.

Predictions
02/16/2008

Their have been many predictions as to who will win this next presidential election. Some voters base their predictions on the qualifications of the candidate. Still others have a liking for the moral character of the candidate. Most canidate's background gives a good indication as to the performance in the White House.

I think that I will focus on Hillary Clinton.

As it stands at this point in time, it appears that she will not be the democratic nominee. Barak Obama has won more primaries she has.

I do not want either of them to win because of their policies.

We have known for years that Hilliary's play was to run for president.

There is one of these Pentecostal ministers, Reverend Perry Stone, PHD, that has given a sermon on the history of the Presidents of the United States. Reverend Stone bases his main idea by the "types and shadows" found in the Bible. What I want to focus on is the idea that he puts forth about the similarities between the Clinton's (Bill and Hillary) and Ahab and Jezebel.

-Ahab and Jezebel lived in an Ivory House.
Bill was elected President.

-Ahab was the leader of th country (Isreal) but Jezabel made the decisions behind the scenes. Enough said.

-Ahab and Jezebel became involved in a land deal.
Bill and Hillary became involved in White Water.

-The land deal fell apart.
Again, enough said.

-Naboth, an innocent man, was killed because of the land deal.
See Vince Foster.

-Jezebel signed papers in Ahab's name concerning the land deal.
Hillary, while working at The Rose Law Firm, signed papers in Bill's name regarding White Water.

-The Bible says that walking in sin was a light for Ahab and Jezebel.
The Clinton's said that his affairs didn't matter because they were in his private life.

-Enemies were raised up against Ahab and Jezebel.

-The true people of God were ridiculed.
The Clinton's vilified what they called religious right.

-There was a forty-two month drought.
There were all kinds of bad weather patterns including drought.

-A lying spirit lied to King Ahab.
The Clinton's said the people who were talking about his affairs were lying.

-Ahab an Jezebel were involved in wars.

-When Ahab was gone, Jezebel was still living in the ivory house.
She is currently running for President.

The line the particular preacher uses is a bible passage (Ecclesiastes 1:9) "The thing that was is the thing that will be, and the thing that is done, is the thing that will be done."

We will see if all of this comes true.

Out Of My Wallet
02/18/2008

In this upcoming election, there are two different sides. One side wants to let you keep the money that you have earned. The other wants to take that money, give in to the government, and have the government redistribute it. This type of thinking flies in the face of the American dream. One comes here as an immigrant to make a better life for himself and his children.

Why was the American Revolution fought?

It was fought because England was overtaxing its colonies.

The democrats feel that to make this a better country they have to tax it to death. The are wrong. They consider themselves "Robin Hoods." They feel this way because they are "stealing from the rich, to give to the poor." The legend of Robin Hood clearly states the reason he was stealing the money was not to give it to the government (king); but, to th people were being overtaxed.

If you look at both of the democratic candidates for president, you will see they want to raise taxes. If that is not bad enough, Barak Obama wants this country to start to pay a tax to the United Nations. If you put that along with the fact the democrats want at least a seventy percent income tax, it is starting to get really scary.

I would like to give them both a message:

GET OUT OF MY WALLET.

Ugliness
02/19/2008

The free-for-all that in the democratic primary is fun to watch. As of this point in time, Obama has a slight lead. The problem is the Clinton's and the underhand schemes they might come up with to get Hillary into the White House.

In the old days, on both sides of the isle, there were the meetings in the smoke filled back room that would decide who the nominee would be. This thing will come down to the delegates and super-delegates. We know the Clinton's can be dirty street brawlers, at times, and they can create things that are not really there. These false things they create, they can make them stick.

They (the Clintons) can break the rules with the best of them. Florida and Michigan had the audacity to change their primaries against the wishes of the party. This was against the rules of the election process. This resulted in their delegates not being seated. Now, what is happening is that both sides want these delegates and are lobbying them for their votes.

If Obama loses out in this lobbying process, the rumor is that he will run as an independent. His vice-presidential candidate is suspected to be Michael Bloomberg, the former Mayor of New York. If this were to happen, one might see the fracturing of the democratic vote; which would lead to the election of John McCain.

This thing will get uglier before it is over.

Stupid Stand
02/20/2008

The United States House of Representatives recently took a, less that tactful, stand against the safety of all Americans when they refused to bring to a vote The Terrorist Surveillance Act. This act would allow the CIA to spy on terrorist who are making phone calls to each other.

The telecommunication industry wants immunity. We all know the democratic party is ruled by the trial lawyers. That is where most of the opposition is coming from. The trial lawyers do not want the telecommunication companies to have immunity because that would be one less person they could sue. It is all a matter of money. The money the trial lawyers could earn, and the money the trial lawyers would give to the democratic party.

This is a very idiotic, stupid stand because it messes with national security.

What Is Support?
02/22/2008

What is meant by the word support? In the congress, support is the subject the military is seeking to continue the fight against terrorism in the Middle East. There may be parts of the military policy the congress may not agree with, but, when a committment is made for peace, there should be a full committment to support the movement with needed equipment and supplies.

The left is still rooted in the war attitudes of the late sixties and early seventies. It will not get better until this current crop of democratic leaders step down. Lawmakers, like Harry Reid and Nancy Pelosi, are great examples of this. Reid said that "the war is lost." Pelosi wanted to go for impeachment, but could not get the job done. Charles Shurmur , at times, has made overtures of trying to impeach the President, Vice President, or someone in this administration. Also, the majority of the professors and academia who are advisors to the democratic lawmakers are from that generation.

It all comes down, to the fact, that these people hate and loathe the military.

Where Is Fidel?
02/23/2008

Back when I was growing up, there was a game called Where's Waldo. The object of the game was to look at a picture of a great number of people and try to fine Waldo. You could probably look at the Fidel Castro situation in much the same way. I really think he is dead, but the higher ups in the Cuban government will not admit it. They do not want to hand the government over to a crazy man like Raoul Castro. If they do, there will be a continuation of holding down the Cuban people.

If there is even a chance that the Cuban people would rise up against this government, then we as the bastion of freedom and democracy should support them as much as we possible can.

Hope and Hopelessness
02/24/2009

In terms of foreign policy, in this upcoming election, there are two distinct patterns of thought. There is the republican ("blue dog" democrat) way of thinking and there is the appeasment (liberal/progressive) method. These two camps have similar views on how to deal with world wide affairs.

There is only one candidate with the neccessesary experiencs to deal with the Islam-O-Fascists. That person is John McCain. He spent several years in the Hanoi Hilton. He has fought a war and knows what it takes to win it, even though he, and the soldiers of his generation were screwed out of a win they rightly deserved. Barak Obama lacks any expierence whatsoever in foreign policy; and Hillary Clinton, a Vietnam war protestor, married to a draft dodger, loathes the military.

McCain has his short comings. On certain issues, he is very liberal, but on most of the important one of our time, he is not. This gives me hope if he is elected. We may very well win this conflict, going away. I have a feeling he will not cut the military the way the two democratic presidents did. I cannot say the same thing about the two candidates on the other side of the isle. McCain knows that, to beat the enemy, we need the best trained, most well equipped soldiers in the history of the world.

The great hope is that McCain gets elected in a landslide over whomerer his opponent is. If his opponent (Clinton or Obama) wins, then the progress we have made in the middle east will go by the wayside. This is where the hopelessness comes into the picture.

No Run?
02/26/2008

Condoleezza Rice has recently said she will not run for either office of President or Vice President. History may have something contrary to say on this matter. She is one of the smartest women in this country. She, unlike Hillary Clinton, is uniquely qualified to hold either post.

She has been the Secretary of State. It is not an unhistorical happening for a former Secretary of State to become, at some point, the President of th United States.

What I am saying is that, I think, if she were asked to serve as the Vice President, she would find it to be an offer she could not refuse.

Step Down
02/27/2008

Even though Fidel Castro has stepped down, it does not mean we should soften our stance on Cuba. Raoul Castro, Fidel's brother, is just as much a lying and a murderous thug his ailing or dead brother is. They have oppressed the Cuban people for too long. If the Cuban exiles in Miami are not happy with this turn of events, the leaders inside or outside of Washington D.C. should not be either.

Until Raoul and the rest of the Cuban Communist party are completely out of power, there is no reason for us to let our guard down.

More On The Loop
02/28/2008

Recently there were some communities that had some questions about the Baton Rouge loop. Some of the questions are very legitimate.

The loop is sorely needed in the Baton Rouge area. It should relieve the traffic problems in the metropolitan area.

Richard Baker's potential hand picked replacement, Paul Sawyer, has said we do not need a loop around the area; but, what should be done is to improve on the current infrastructure.

The rest of the candidates, basically, agree it is needed and that it should be built.

This is an important election for the Baton Rouge area. We have a lot of our national legislators retiring and we need to put the correct people in office so we can get the federal monies, with no strings attached to complete this loop.

Kosovo Constitution
02/29/2008

The Kosovars have declared their freedom. As human beings it is their right to do so. The problem is that others will try to tell them what they can include in their constitution. Whatever they write into it should be their choice, not someone from the outside. If they do not want to give women freedom, that is their choice. If there is a section specifically written to prohibit homosexuals to practice their lifestyle, so be it. There are hundreds or thousands of things they could put into the document that will possibly be there for the perpetuity of time. That choice should be left up to them.

GOP Vice President Possibilities
03/01/08

We do not have any idea who John McCain will pick as his Vice President running mate. We are not in his head.

There are many people he could choose who will make good candidates.

01. Mark Sanford (S. CAROLINA)
02. Tim Pawlenty (MINNESOTA)
03. Mel Martinez (FLORIDA)
04. Michael Steele (MARYLAND)
05. Rick Santorum (PENNSYLVANIA)
06. Duncan Hunter (CALIORNIA)
07. Condolezza Rice (CALIFORNIA)

Sanford, Pawlenty, Hunter, and Santorum are white men whose conservative credentials are beyond reproach. They are all younger than McCain. Hunter, like McCain, is a Vietnam War veteran. It would be very hard to get to Hunter on the war, because his son is currently on the front lines in Iraq. Sanford and Pawlenty have been conservative governors and know how to run the ship of state. Pawlenty has an extra added plus, because he has ruled in a, mostly, liberal state. Santorum, in the senate, had been one of the most conservative people in the congress.

Because of his stance on immigration, it makes all the since in the world that he would ask Mel Martinez to be his vice president mate.

If Barak Obama wins the democratic nomination, it would make since to have an African-American on the GOP ticket. Michael Steele and Condoleeza Rice makes sense. They are both articulate. They both know what it is like to be an African-American politician in America. The only question I have is weather or not Ms. Rice will be as conservative on fiscal policy as she is on national security.

We do not know who McCain will choose. OR, will it be someone else?

Unlimited
03/02/2008

There could be an unprecedented amount of petroleum left in the world. This flies in the face of the people that oil alarmists say we will run out of oil within the next couple hundred years.

Giora Proskurowski, a scientist that studies such things, has said as much. This scientist has said the earth continually renews the petroleum that has been taken away from it. The earth does this from the crust itself. Now, don't get me wrong, it doesn't do this in the form of oil; but in the form of methane. Methane is the unrefined version of natural gas. If there is a way for us to fix it, such that automobiles would run on natural gas, there is a chance we would not have to depend on our enemies for oil supplies. This is the ultimate goal.

Bombing the Mountains
03/03/2008

I am favor of bombing the mountains of Waziristan, Pakistan to the ground. I recently read an article about the United States military firing missiles at selected targets in that particular area in Pakistan. If they continue these, there is a great chance lady luck will be on their side and either Osama Bin-Laden or Ayman Al-Zawhiri will be killed.

This is exactly the type of things that need to happen for us to continue to win the war on terror.

Are we really sure that either Hillary Clinton or Barak Obama will have the will to continue this type of attack?

We will soon see.

Big Time Up-And-Coming
03/04/2008

There may very well be some distance for Louisiana's Governor Bobby Jindal to go on the ethics road. This first series of bills is a nice start. This may have move the ball down the political field somewhere between ten and forty-five yards. He, also, has to deal with the states business and tax structure. If Jindel can straighten this state out, then he can write his own ticket politically.

The man is young, energetic, and politically savvy. He may, very well, be the future of the Republican party. Should he not win a second term as governor, he will come out of this having a great deal of political, legislative, and executive ruling experience before he turns forty-five years old.

The other GOP hopefuls, Sanford, Barbour, and Pawlenty will be four to eight years older. This means they will be in their mid fifties; whereas, Jindal will be in his mid forties. Therefore, he will be like Barak Obama, except he will have the experience.

He could be a Godsend for the republican party.

He is to Louisiana like Arnold Schwartzenegger was in California; before he got elected to his first term.

Agreement
03/05/2008

With all of the positives coming out of Iraq, I agree with Angelina Jolie that it is now safe enough to start sending in humanitarian aid on a great scale. Because of the war, there are many Iraqi people who are displaced to other countries around the middle east. It is now time for then to go home to a better life.

Because of Saddam Hussein, the Iraq people's lives were made a living hell.

Jolie is right when she says we should not squander the military progress made in Iraq. We are one of the most giving countries in the world and at this time we are the only ones who can give.

Miss Jolie better be careful as to what she says. Should she continue withe comments about the war she could fall out of favor with her Hollywood elite liberal "friends".

Slaps On The Wrist
03/06/2008

Sometimes, there are disciplinary groups that do not go far enough in the punishment doled out to offenders. This is frustrating to the people who have hired them to monitor the running of the organization.

The Federal Elections Commission is supposed to come down hard on elected officials, on the national stage, that have broken the law.

If an elected official misreports campaign funds, he should be slapped down hard. These types of law breakages need to be treated like the end of the world. If they are treated in this manner, the punishments doled out would mean something. The punishments would be good enough to, not only make the current offender think about not doing it again, but it would make others seriously think about breaking the laws.

Thirty Years At War
03/07/2008

We have been at war with radical Islam since 1979. It all stared when President Jimmy Carter messed around in the politics of Iran. In doing this, he gave us the Ayatollah Khomeini and ultimately Mahmoud Ahmadinihad. In doing this, it led directly to the Iran Hostage Crisis.

There were a few issues in the 1980's with radical Islam. It started with the bombing of our embassies in Africa. Then came the bombings in India. Next up, was the first attack against the World Trade Center. It was, then, followed by the blowing up of the USS Cole.

Finally, came the day that changed the world, 9/11. Look, I may have missed some of the attacks against us; but those were the main ones that really matter. They prove we have been at war with these idiots, that make good Muslims look bad, for almost thirty years.

Presidential Prediction
03/08/2008

President George W. Bush has predicted there will be a republican president. I hope he is right. I do think the Republicans will gain a few seats in congress, but it will not be enough to give them congress. I do think it will be enough to block any attempt the democrats may take to override a presidential veto. We need this to happen for the ability to stop any of the crazy things that are sure to come out of this liberal democratic congress.

I sure hope this prediction comes true.

Still At It
03/09/2008

The State of Louisiana is still at it. All of this states major legislators from Governor Bobby Jindal to Senator 'Katrina' Mary Landrieu are lobbying to have a presidential debate to happen in New Orleans.

The excuse given is that the "Big Easy" can not handle it because the city has not recovered enough. This is a complete falsehood. Ask the National Basketball Association about the "egg on its face" after it said New Orleans could not handle the All-Star Game. Year-in and year-out the city handles nearly one million people for Mardi Gras. Do they not know how many Super Bowls have taken place in this city? Do not even mention the way the city has handled the Sugar Bowl, Bayou Classic, Final Fours, and the countless number of concerts and convention.

It is probably time for a "Hail Mary" (not Mary Landrieu) in trying to get a presidential debate. It can't hurt to try. We have always been told that she is listening. (Again, not Mary Landrieu, she never listens to the people.)

What Else Needs Doing
03/10/2008

We have taken a good first step in correcting some of the ethics and corruptions problems in the state of Louisiana. What is next to be done? The answer is to make this a more business friendly state. How do we do that? There are many ways.

Get rid of the many taxes an fees that are hurting the state. The income tax needs to go. Things like the Stelley Bill needs to be thrown overboard. The redefinition of taxes and fees needs to be erased from the states 'dictionary'.

We, the people of Louisiana, need to keep getting rid of the dregs of the old guard that remain in the state legislature.

If we keep on the same track we are on, the other major things that remain will get done. The roads will get fixed, education will get fixed, and the best and the brightest of our young people will stop moving out of the state and the ones that have gone will come back.

Cry, Cry Again
03/12/2008

The teachers' unions in the state of Louisiana need to stop their crying. We have passed taxes upon taxes to get their pay up to a competitive level. We have also passed taxes to help in the up keep and building of schools.

There is a bill that was passed by the Louisiana House of Representatives that would, essentially, help the people who are getting it "put to them" twice with schooling. They have made the decision to send their kids to private, parochial, or home school. This bill will be a tuition tax credit. It will give the amount of three-hundred dollars to those choosing other than public education. These people are paying their taxes, but are going in another educational direction, because it appears the public schools are not substancially improving. They have decided to send their children to private/parochial school or to keep at home and home school them.

The teachers' unions can lobby for raises in salary and up keep in the conditions of schools, but that should be it. Their arguments is it will harm the public schools system in the state and the schools may fall flat on their faces. That is a total bold face lie. There are kids who will go to the public schools. There are kids who will go to private or parochial school. There are parents who will choose to keep their kids home and home school them. What this law will do is to help low income parents who want to send their kids to a better school environment, but would not be able to afford it.

It can not be argued that public school students can not succeed. Even the inner city school have become places where the hearts, spirits, and minds of the students are flourishing.

Arbitron Stinks
03/13/2008

Arbitron is a rating company that helps radio stations determine programming. They tell the stations their options for the kinds of programming for the listening audiance.

Sometime some stations trust Arbitron too much.

February started a ratings period for radio stations. This is a time when station, if they are in the talk radio format, try to get "new and different callers." The service may work with nationally syndicated radio shows and regional radio shows, but it just does not fly with local shows. Local shows have a smaller listener ship. They cover a certain area, and that is it. In terms of trying to get "new callers", in my opinion, just does not happen. If a station is in a city like Baton Rouge, it may be drawing from a big pool of potential listeners and callers. A radio station may reach more than a couple of thousand listeners, but the number of people calling into the stations is greatly dwarfed by the amount of listeners.

If there is a host that has a two-hour show, less than one percent of the people listening will actually call. Of that less than one percent, most of those callers are, what I term as, "consistent callers." These "consistent callers" are the people that call on a day-in-day-out basis. Why would you want to turn these types of callers away?

There is a certain station (WJBO) that will not allow a certain person (your humble blogger) to become a consistent caller on their programs. I don't blame some of the hosts. It all comes from the program director or "Monkey", as a nationally syndicated host (Jim Rome) says. He calls them monkeys because he thinks, and rightly so, if you take a monkey from a zoo and put him in that job, it will do just as good of a job. I tend to agree with that. I think even if radio stations do not agree with a caller, the caller should be allowed to express his views. In listening to WJBO, I can hear some of the same people calling everyday. They tell me not to call but other daily callers are allowed to call as many times as they want. How fair is this? Even though it may not be this way, it appears they are singling me out because of my stand on certain issues. I have built up my name recognition on sports radio, why can't I do the same thing on news talk radio? If there are 20 callers in a given show, I would say eighty percent (16 callers) of the people that call are the same regular calling people. You may only get four new callers in a given show.

It is wrong for them to do this to a caller that people would tune in to listen to.

What Will an Obama Presidency Mean for the War on Terror?
03/14/2008

A great majority of terrorist leaders think that a Barak Obama presidency will be a positive for the global Jihad movement.

Unless he changes his mind on some of his foreign policy, these people might be dead on correct. Obama wants to negotiate win Iran. That would be mistake number one. He would run away from Israel. He would withdraw troops very quickly. It took our military twenty years to get back the respect that it lost in Vietnam. We do not want to have to go through that again.

The term 'War On Terror' would disappear.

It would be a very bad four to eight years for American foreign policy.

Trouble Being a Frontrunner
03/15/2008

There are definite drawbacks to being a frontrunner in any election.

The person that is behind, usually, is a desperate campaigner who will stoop to dirty politics.

These types of campaigns are the ones that try to use the other persons religion. Some people accuse others of being racist. There are many other dirty tricks that happen in every election cycle.

Sure, the republicans run dirty tricks, but the democrats are excellent at it. One of their presidential candidates, Hillary Clinton, and her husband, are two of the dirtiest campaigners in the history of American politics. They use such things like private investigators in their campaigns to try to "dig up dirt" on opposing candidates.

Being a frontrunner is a dangerous thing.

What Might Be
03/16/2008

When former general and war hero Dwight D. Eisenhower became president, he became a person of peace. He became this type of person because he saw the horrors of war.

John McCain may, very well, be the mold. Sure, he was held as a POW in Vietnam, but he may not want any of our soldiers to go through the same things he has gone through. He has a new doctrine to try to enforce, and I will wager he will use the Bush Doctrine when he absolutely has to.

Jason Raimondo thinks John McCain will go overboard in using, and defending the Bush Doctrine. Yes, McCain has fashioned himself as a maverick. This does not mean he will be as hawkish as Mr. Raimondo thinks he will be.

McCain, at times, has been loved by the "drive-by" media. He has purposely done this so that he can get favorable press. The problem with what McCain has done is the drive-by's are starting to turn on him.

Back to Mr. Raimondo. It is obvious that he is a liberal and he has turned against his 'buddy' John McCain. He criticizes McCain for saying there should be more boots on the ground, even though Senator McCain was right. He was right in Iraq just as he was right with the same comments he uttered when American troopos went into Kosovo.

The President of the United States is a prime time player. You have to have a big ego to think you can make the right decisions, at the correct time, that will eventually affect everyone in the world.

I think that he could be a good president. The question will not be with his foreign policy but with his domestic policy, especially his energy policy.

Total Destruction
03/17/2008

If the Clintons decide to try to steal election from Barak Obama, it will definitely hurt the democratic party.

If there are some conservative blacks who voted for the dems in elections, those people will switch over to the republican side.

If the Clintons carry through with this, it will wreck their party for a couple of decades. They may need this to happen for the people that should be in charge too get back into power. The current crop of power brokers in that party may be too far left for the "Joe six-pack democrat." This party needs a true blue dog, conservative, southern democrat to step up and take the party back. HillaryClinton and Barak Obama are not this type of democrat.

Will the take back happen anytime soon?

I don't think so.

Black Leaders Could Cost Obama
03/18/2008

Barak Obama is running for the office of the President of the United States. He is the first black American to be a legitimate candidate. I use the term black American because he was not born in Africa and he grew up in the America.

I don't know what is going on with the black American leaders. They need to shut up, because. if they do not, they might possibly cost Obama his chance at being president. People like Ray "Chocolate City" Nagin, Kwame Kilpatrick, William "Cold Cash" Jefferson, Cynthia McKinnie, and others, by their words and actions may harm Obama's chances.

Barak Obama, even though I do not agree with him on most of his policies, is a "gen-x'er". He may be the best shot at changing their party and getting past the old farts who are currently leading the democratic party. The party needs to put the Clinton's in their past, along withe Jesse Jackson, Al Sharpton and other black liberal leaders. If they don't, it could be a great chance it will rip the democratic party apart; and, they may not be able to put it back together again for at least one generation.

What Is Meant
03/19/2008

The Washington D.C. gun law case is coming up in the Supreme Court. The citizens of D.C. can not own a handgun; and if they own a rifle, it has to be disassembled if they are to keep the gun in the house. That is just not right and not at all feasible. If a person is at home and is being threatened, he may need to get a fully put together gun to be able to protect yourself.

This case will come down to how the justices interpret the constitution. You have some very liberal judges on the Supreme Court and they are for gun laws like the Brady Bill. It will all come down to how certain justices make there arguments to convince the "middle of the road" justices to come over to their side.

I would very much like to see some of the gun laws rolled back.

There are three decisions that could could be reached. These are them:

1. They could rule the laws stay as is.

2. They could rule the gun law is unconstitutional and all guns are legal.

3. They can make it a narrow ruling and say it applies only to Washington D.C.

It all depends on what the justices interpert what is meant by certain words in the second amendment of the U.S. Constitution.

The Visit
03/20/2008

Recently, presidential hopeful John McCain visited Iraq. McCain has been in favor of the was in Iraq. There has been some minor procedural issues on the war, as it has progressed. I agree, there has been slight issues on the prosecution of other wars; but this war needed to happen.

It is true that McCain's bid for the presidency is tied to whether we are successful in the war in Iraq. Part of his platform is national security and a major factor is his big time support for the war in Iraq. As long as we remain successful, his bid will remain strong.

We really can not afford for either one of the democratic hopefuls to win the battle for the White House, even though I don't think either Hillary Clinton or Barak Obama will pull out of the race. If one of these democratic candidates wins the White House, look for a cut in funding for the Pentagon. Not having money for the military will give a good excuse for our country to pull out of the war.

Watch Their Backs
03/21/2008

Heath Shuler, a freshman democratic senator from the state of North Carolina, has proposed a bill that would add another eight thousand border protection agents. The GOP has filed a discharge petition. This is a procedural ploy by the republicans. It is designed to get a bill to the floor for a vote.

Heath Shuler and other conservative democrats should watch their backs. The leaders of the democratic party may say they will not go after these congressmen in the primary, but I don't trust them. The democratic party is a party of retribution. They can put undo pressure on senators or representatives who do not vote the way the democratic party leaders want them to vote. I fear for Heath Shuler, and other democrats like him. He, probably, should have run as a republican.

If Hillary Clinton should happen to win, watch for the retribution. The reason is that a big part of her voting block is the Hispanic lobby. She needs to be defeated..

Johnson, On Trial As Well As Odom
03/22/2008

We all know how crooked Bob Odom has been. If you think that it ended here, you are wrong. His honor, Judge Don Johnson has allowed himself to be drawn into the tentacles of the giant squid named Bob Odom. He is just as crooked as Odom. He allowed his friendship with Odom to color how he adjudicated the trial against his buddy.

It is as simple as the day to day running of the "Good Ole Boy" network. Friends helping friends, and cronies helping cronies. Odom got the trial of his long term friend assigned to his court. He had the authority to have all of the charges dismissed. He did that.

In my opinion, what needs to happen is for the Louisiana Court of Appeals to reverse all of the charges and there should be a change of venue and judge.

Founded Anger
03/23/2008

Keavin Keith, a resident of Iberville Parish and City of Plaquemine, is rightfully angry at the national government for not defending the borders.

I understand his anger. The problem with it is that he said "Let them move their businesses to Mexico." That is a wrong headed felling because these plants are a big part of the state's economy. Without them, we would have a third world economy.

Mister Keith also needs to understand that this a necessary evil. It is a correctable evil but the politicians don't want to correct it.

Is The NIE a LIE?
03/24/2008

When the National Intelligence Estimate came out in late 2007, it said that Iran had stopped making weapons' grade uranium and plutonium. That does not mean they have not started it up again.

Most of the countries in that region are deathly afraid of a nuclear Iran. A nuclear Iran, automatically, becomes the big bully in the middle east. It also means the good countries will have to go nuclear. That makes for a scarey situation.

The NIE is, for the most part, a lie. The democrats have "cherry picked" information that suit their purposes. They focused on certain information they thought would stop President George W. Bush from bombing Iran, while on his way out of the White House.

Do Conservatives Really Want A Big Tent?
03/25/2008

I do not know what is wrong with the GOP. It has seemed that it has lost its way. It wants as many people in the movement and party as it can possibly have. That theory is definitely hurting what conservatives are trying to do. The more liberal a republican person professes to be, the harder it is to pass conservative policies.

Yes, there are some people who are not conservative enough. There are reasons they are this way. On some issues, they are conservative but because of where they are from, there are some issues they will be a bit more liberal on.

The deal is this; we, as conservatives, will have to put up with "liberal" republicans. I hope it does not drag the party into a direction that there is no difference between the GOP and the democratic party.

Somebody "Save" The Border
03/26/2008

Nancy Pelosi and the liberal wing of the democratic party are at it again. They still want to grant amnesty to illegal aliens. That is why Heath Shuler's Save Act has not and will not see the light of day.

This is a bill that aims to protect the borders first, and later, be able to wrangle over the other, more liberal parts of the "comprehensive" immigration bill. The democratic liberals being greedy, immature, and stupid.

This is the reason why the approval rating of congress is at an all time low.

Ambition Can Be A Good Thing
03/27/2008

Ambition is and, of itself, can be either a good thing or a bad thing. If one is ambitious it can be bad if he has to climb over others to get where he is going.

In wanting to clean up the State of Louisiana, Governor Bobby Jindal is showing positive ambition.

The State Of Louisiana, for the longest time, has been nothing less than a cesspool. It has been known as one of th worst states to do business in. There has been an out-migration problem. This means our best and brightest have been leaving the state at an alarming rate. There is the "Louisiana Misery Index", which states all of the areas we are last in; and it is not a small list. Our taxes are way too high. We are so awashed in political double talk that we can't tell if we are coming or going. The worst thing is the corruption.

The "Good Ole Boy" network has ruled this state far too long.

It might be too much to ask for Jindal to attempt to clean up, but he is going to go ahead and try. It will probably take a series of reform minded governors to get the job done. Governor Jindal is a nice start.

Correction Of The Market
03/28/2008

We have seen the housing market on a "bubble" for some times now. There are people that want the government to correct it. That is the wrong way to go about it. The government needs to stay out of the business world. The problem is not greedy CEO's, but, it is the government that does not understand economy and the CEO's objectives. The company hires him to do a job and he deserves all he can get from his legal contract.

The government wants to control everything that a business does. That is fascism. That is getting into an area promoted by Hitler, Mussolini, and Hugo Chavez. These foreign country leaders controled and are controlling the businesses inside the borders of their countries.

That is not the right direction to go in our economic democracy.

What needs to happen is for us to let the housing "bubble" correct itself, even if it is a drag on the economy.

Nice Start
03/29/2008

Governor Bobby Jindal ran on a reform platform. He won the election with over fifty percent of the state's vote. He has been given a powerful mandate by the people of Louisiana, who are expressing to him that this state is sick and tired of being sick and tired.

For too long, we have had some of the worst, most corrupt politicians in the nation; and for a long time, we refused to correct the problem. We, as a state, have dealt with people like Edwin W. Edwards and others. We have sent several insurance commissioners to jail. Also, we have elected people to the legislature that have had enough character flaws to allow them to become corrupt.

In the last special session, Jindal got passed what he could get passed. He still has a great deal of distance to go. He couldn't get into a big fight because it would have spent a great deal of his political capital needed to get some tax reform passed.

Will he get everything that he wants?

Not in this session.

How long will it take for him to get what he wants?

I don't know.

Will outside forces conspire to not allow him to get done what he wants to get done?

We will see.

Is It A Good Idea?
03/31/2008

Iberville now has an Academy, which will open in the next school session. This Academy will, specifically, target students who show a high proficiency in math, science, and the arts. It will be available for all student throughout the parish. It will start with students in the seventh grade and include eighth and ninth graders. Other grades will be added in future years.

Will this progtam help to keep the more accelerated students in those specific subjects in the public schools?

I don't know.

I tend to believe that it will keep those students in the Iberville Parish public schools, at least until the parents can determine if this program is worthwhile to the educational growth of their children.

Who Is Your Candidate?
04/01/2008

Who will win the election? Who is your candidate? The answers to those questions will occur in eight months. Some say all three candidates are the same person. I am not sure about that. I think McCain is more conservative. He has said he wants to lower taxes, appoint conservative judges, and have a strong military.

Could he be another Gerald R. Ford? That is a possibility. We will have to see if he can find a way to win against what might be a democratic dominated congress. Can he be either George W Bush or Ronald Reagan. It seems like Bush has so out maneuvered the democrats that they continue to open the door on their collective noses. President Reagan talked over the congresses heads directly to the American people.

Hillary Clinton and Barak Obama, in terms of their policies, are the same candidate. This is why they are beating each others brains out with the other subjects.

We will see if McCain can overcome the perceived albatross the democrats believe George W. Bush is.

Teaching
04/02/2008

It now appears that a Louisiana legislator wants to try to fight the fight on creationism/intelligent design in schools. I have been waiting a long time for this.

Senator Ben Nevers (D-Bogalusa) wants to teach this alternative view of the scientific past of our planet.

He says "Students should be exposed to both sides of the scientific data and that they should be allowed to make up their own minds."

The people against that are trotting out the age old argument of separation of church and state. Barry Lynn says "This is all about God in biology class."

Senator Nevers' bill is called the "Louisiana Academic Freedom Act."

It states that:

Educational authorities should "Assist teachers to find more effective ways to present the scientific curriculum where it addresses scientific controversies."

Biological evolution, global warming, and other topics "can cause controversy," in public school classrooms and confuse teachers as to what should be taught.

Teachers and others should encourage students to tackle different views on such topics, which include scientific strengths and weaknesses of each theory.

I agree with Senator Nevers' in theory, but it is going to be difficult to put into practice. Liberal groups like Americans United for the Separation of Church and State are going to oppose it.

Those type of people want the status quo.

Even if it is passes, it will be taken to court and fought tooth and nail. I think it will survive due to the fact their are more conservatives on the Supreme Court.

Waterlogged
04/03/2008

In this country the most vulnerable places for terrorists' attacks are the seaports. It is just a matter of time before the bad guys find a way to bring weapons into this country from the sea and destroy our seaports.

Here is what could happen:

1. A ship with hundreds of very large containers could steams into a port.

2. Because there are so few people at the docks to search these containers, there is a definite possibility that, not only terrorists, but, equipment could slip through.

3. The terrorists could take the equipment and assemble it into a bomb.

4. It could be taken to a city like Minneapolis and a facility like the Mall of the Americas could be destroyed.

At the time of the attack, the mall could be at its capacity and there would be thousands of innocents people killed.

Against Strategic Defense
04/04/2008

China is a progressively growing country. Their military is getting to a point which can rival America's military. That is a scary thought.

The Chinese are afraid of America having the Strategic Defense Initiative or Star Wars. China's missile technology is getting more advanced and they are advancing to the ability to have long rage ballistic rockets. They want the ability to attack America and her allies with impunity and immunity.

If you believe in the battle of Armageddon, as I do, then this should really attrack your attention..

Medicare is Medi-Scare
04/05/2008

Medicare is running out of money. If its problem does not get corrected there will not be the ability for the government to cover the medical expenses of the retirees that will be retiring in the next ten to twenty years.

Retired citizens need to have the ability to have their medical needs attended to is the twilight of their lives.

Our government can correct this problem. They can get rid of the payroll tax. They can lessen the income tax to the point which it would not hurt employers. These employers could continue to keep employees on their payroll, thus, continuing the amount contributing into the medicare pool.

Will our lawmakers be smart enough to take these precautions?

I am not sure.

Is It Over?
04/06/2008

The two special legislative sessions Governor Bobby Jindal recently called were very successful. The majority of what he wanted to get done got done. This lead some people to speculate there was a "honeymoon" taking place.

Now that those special sessions are over, the democratic majority in the legislature is blowviating about how the Governor's honeymoon is over. It might just be. We may see that he will appoint people, as leaders, that are favorable to his policies. If he can get enough moderate democrats to cross the isle, he will continue to get his policies enacted. That is the rub. He is going to have "schmooze" those moderates for them to stay on his side.

The question is: Just how many of those moderate democrats were elected?

Also, needing to be asked is: How many "new" republicans will defect if he pushes to hard?

Serious Seeking
04/07/2008

Condoleeza Rice is seriously lobbying for the vice presidential spot on the ticket with Senator John McCain.

She would make a pretty go choice because, not only does she have the experience in foreign policy but she would help to counter balance the effect of Barak Obama.

If she is on the ticket, and McCain ends up getting more the fifteen percent of the votes, he could end up blowing out either democratic candidate Obama or Hillary Clinton.

It makes good sense. She is an name that a republicans throughout the country know. Even though I would like to see Governor Bobby Jindal get a fair shot at the position, he is not quit ready for prime time.

There needs to be some serious questions answered by Dr. Rice. The most important of these questions is her feelings on things like tax policies. She needs to prove how conservative she really is.

I would, not at all, have any problem with her succeeding John McCain if something, Lord forbid, were to happen to him.

What If?
04/09/2008

Bob Barr, A former United States Representative, is considering a third party run for the office of the president. This man is a true conservative.

What would probably happen is Mr. Barr would draw conservatives away from John McCain. Would this lead to a Hillary Clinton or Barak Obama presidency? It is hard to say because Ralph Nader is, also in the mix. Both Clinton and Obama will have to try to move to the center. Nader will stake his claim to the far left and possibly draw enough votes away from Clinton or Obama to gum up the works. Even though there is a general feeling the conservatives republicans have migrated around McCain, they may not be happy he is actively trying to win the independents to his side.

Mr. Barr, if anything else, would bleed conservatives away for McCain. This would cause the, already, low voter turnout to be a fractured one. This could cause the result of the election to look like this:

Winner: 41%
Loser #1: 39%
Loser #2: 10%
Loser #3: 10%

This means the top vote getter would not come close to having a mandate and would end up being a weak president.

What's In A Surplus?
04/10/2008

It seems like every so often the state of Louisianan has budget surpluses. As the surpluses come up, there are arguments on how to spent them. The problem with such arguments is that they are made by politicians; and usually do not include giving the money back to the people.

The point of this matter is that this money is the peoples money collected from taxes from the good folks of this state. It should be given back.

What usually happens is that these people in the legislature find a way to screw the people out of the surplus money, which is rightfully theirs. This money SOMEHOW finds its way into pet projects and earmarks.

We, the people, want our money back.

Money Back
04/11/2008

Louisiana is an overtaxed state. Thanks to previous legislatures redefining old terms and coming up with new ones, we have been contributing increasing amounts of tax money to the state government. We, as the tax paying public, have allowed this to happen. It is time, we, the people, of the state of Louisiana, get fed up about this situation.

It will not get better unless we get active and force our senators and representatives to do what needs to be done.

We, as their bosses, may need to change some of our legislators if they refuse to do what we want.

As it has been said before, this is a multiple election cycle. If the current crop of politicians don't want to "know their roll," then we must "shut their mouths."

Tighten Up
04/12/2008

It seems both of the democratic contenders for the President of the United States are running, somewhat, undisciplined campaigns.

Hillary Clinton keeps allowing her husband, Bill, to make statements that appear to stall any momentum she seems to be getting.

Barak Obama, on the other hand, keeps having to defend himself on things like his controversial pastor and the William Ayers issues.

If things like this keep coming up in both of these campaigns, it will not only hurt them in the democratic primary, but it will damage their chances in the general election. This could lead to John McCain being elected President of the United States.

Why Should He?
04/13/2008

John McCain is jumping Barak Obama's case about saying he is thinking about not taking public matching funds should he become the democratic nominee for the White House.

I can see where McCain is coming from on this issue. If Obama says he is going to take public funds and he does not; then, he is going to appear to be a liar. He will, also, look like your typical politician who says one thing and does another.

On the other hand, why should he accept the rules regarding public funding? It states that the candidate can spend no more than $85 million dollars. The fact is that Obama can raise more than that on the internet. Why should he limit himself to a certain amount?

We are now in a different era. This is the era of the Generation Xers. This is the era of the internet and McCain is from a different era. Even though I don't like Obama's policies, I have to give it to him. He has found ways to raise staggering amounts of money in other legal ways other than the normal "old school" ways.

What's In a Win
04/14/2008

A win is a win, is it not? Benchmarks met are benchmarks met, are they not? To the democrats, those two statements are not what they are. Sometimes appearances are deceiving, but in this case they are not.

The loser-crats are still at it trying to lose the war. It seems like every time General Petreaus and Ambassador Crocker comes back with, somewhat, good news, those who want to see America look bad and lose the war, see their chances of that happening go further and further down the toilet. They, also, see their hopes of a major "clog in the pipes" less likely to happen; and they are acting like little babies because of it.

Generally, the American people do not like their lawmakers to act this way. American people are like sports fans. They want to see their team, the American military, win.

The democrats, on the other hand, do not want and can not allow that to happen. If they do, it might cost them the election. They absolutely know this is the case.

As has been said before, "Anything good for the country (America), is bad for the democratic party."

Hoaxers Hurt
04/15/2008

The Church of Environmentalism's hoax of global warming is hurting the country. I call it a church because there is a priest-reverened (Al Gore) and deacons (environmental groups) that keep this idiotic hoax alive.

This "religion" is hurting the country. Because it has been so successful, it has curtailed the drilling for, and the reining of oil in the greater forty-eight states of this fine nation. What it has, also, done is it has put our national security at risk. Because we can not drill, we have to get our oil from other places. Most of those places are from other countries and regions of the world, mainly the Middle East.

This creates a dangerous situation for our country because we have to deal with the radical Islamists. If one of those groups should get the boldness to go out and attack the oil wells in Saudi Arabia, we might, very well, be in serious trouble.

If we don't reign these people in, they will end up destroying the greatness of the shining city on the hill.

Inferior
04/16/2008

The leftist of the world, including the American democrats, are governing with fear and are making the people feel inferior. In the words of Rush Limbaugh, "All they (the democrats) have to offer is fear itself."

What fears, you may ask? Well, the fear of money, or lack of it, if the American people lose their jobs and cannot pay for their homes. The fear the military will not be successful in the Middle East. The fear of racism caused by inequality in some areas of our society. The fear of economic progress, and may others. This fear of economic progress is brought on by the politicians who do not want our country to be an oil rich nation, not depending on foreign oil supplies.

Look at the people who "race-bait" the American people. Activist like Al Sharpton and Jessie Jackson do not want the race issue to go away. If it did, there goes their business.

The democrats are trying to block the true American dream. This dream is to come to this country as an immigrant, make yourself successful and make life better for your successive generations. Democrats are trying to convince people they can get rich by the government redistributing the wealth; meaning to take away from someone who has become successful by hard work and sacrifices, and give it to people who have not earned their way. They do this through TAXES.

They want communism/fascism.

To that end, they will do anything it takes to keep the normal, working class people down.

MFP 3:16: I am correct and you know it.

Things Just Don't Seem To Get Done
04/17/2008

Louisiana politicians seem to want to exhaust the people. Ideas that seem to be good ideas drag on and on and seem to never get done. Other things that seem to be greedy and self-serving get done and finished in record time.

The way ideas get hatched and carried out beats down on the people of the state of Louisiana and discourages them. It makes the young people who would be the greatness and the future of the state not want to be here. In doing that, it makes them want to move away and not want to come back.

The "baggy pants" issue is one that seems to be moving at a "snail's pace". A good and firm law about this could clean up the communities of the reprobates; but it seems to be hard to get a law passed

For some reason we can not seem to find the money to pay our debts. There is suppose to be money in the budget to pay both the Hornets and the Saints subsidies. It seems to not be there. It would be be there if we were not paying for such things like unpaid rounds of golf, and unneeded lakes and reservoirs.

Don't even get me started on the whole motorcycle helmet issue. Why can't we have a hard and fast law, and stick to it?

Until our politicians change, things will not get better.

Ties To The Past
04/18/2008

General Bennett Landraneau may be a good person with the correct qualifications to be the head of the Louisiana National Guard, but his political ties to the past is the way he is about to get the job.

His recomendation for the position appears to be a suggestion from a former governor. That is the way things have been done in the past. Why is Governor Bobby Jindal not doing research and making this important hire independently of what former Governor Mike Foster thinks? Or, is the general due a political favor.

This whose situation reeks of how things were done in the past in the state of Louisiana.

Rejects Can Be Stars
04/19/2008

When your friends kick you out of a club or organization you have been in for your whole life, it hurts. Just ask Joe Lieberman. Senator Lieberman had been a lifelong democrat. When he sided with President George W. Bush over the war, the democrats basically disowned him. This forced him to become an independent.

It now appears that he has enough friends on the other side of the aisle that he may be able to speak at the Republican National Convention.

Dick "Turbin" Durbin and Harry "the war is lost" Reid have said that if Lieberman is asked, and decides to speak at the Republican National Convention, Lieberman would lose his chairmanship. I do not trust them as far as I can throw them. That whole party is a mean, vindictive party. If he crosses them on this issue, he might, very well, see the party try to take away his seat or force him to retire.

If he is asked by Senator John McCain to be a speaker, it will take an extreme amount of guts for him to step up and do it.

Anybody Can Run For Anything
04/20/2008

If one feels issues are not going in the right direction, politically, he can run for office and try to change things.

It does not matter what one does for a living, if he shows a seriousness and sincereness in running for office, he should have a fair shot at being elected.

Even if there are some issues a person disagrees with, that should not stop him from seeking the office.

After all, that is the American way.

Abandonment
04/21/2008

President Ronald Reagan once said, "There are some people of Israeli descent the democratic party has abandoned".

If the democratic party, as it is now constituted, were around during World War II, there might still be a genocide against the Jewish people.

If President Franklin Roosevelt would have had the present-day congress they would have opposed him to go to war. If America had not been allowed to get into the war, even after the heinous attack on Pear Harbor, the Nazis takeover of Europe would have been left unchecked; as would the Imperial Japanese takeover of Southeast Asia. Without us, the Russians might have lost as well.

Those thoughts are scary ones.

Most Jews in America identify themselves as being democrats and liberal because of what happened to their families in Europe during the late 1930's and early 1940's.

The problem today is that the democrats are now consciously avoiding the fight against evil in the world.

That just won't do.

I am not saying a great majority of Jews will vote for John McCain or other republicans, but there could just be enough that would swing the election and the congress in a direction to make a difference.

Elitists Are Just That
04/22/2008

Real Americans are not elitists. They are the people who live, for the most part, in small towns, any-town USA. They are the people who are forgotten by the snobbish, elite people that Barak Obama and Hillary Clinton hang out with. Clinton may, very well be just as elitist as Obama, but she is not dumb enough to state it publicly. She knows if she makes those types of statements her candidacy would be hurt as badly as Obams's is being hurt.

When you have pockets of people whose jobs dry up or move out, then you can understand how they can get frustrated with the ruling class.

Obama does not understand that being religious is a good thing. It is one of the only things that keeps the people in these tougher parts of the country sane.

As far as guns are concerned, that is another issue. That is a constitutional issue. It is also a historical issue in places like the state of Pennsylvania. There, the history is that of the Revolution and the fight for freedom of the original thirteen colonies.

This is just another way for Obama and others like him to try to denigrate the term redneck.

The Destruction Of A Party On The All Important Issue Of National Defense
04/23/2008

Whatever national security credentials the democratic party has accrued over the history of the country, has been eroded during the last forty years.

Ever since Vietnam the democrats have developed a yellow streak and it has consistently grown larger. For some reason, it has emboldened the democrats to say more and more idiotic things. They are acting in ways that have hurt our military troops; who are couragously fighting for truth, freedom and the American way.

What would Andrew Jackson, FDR, Harry Truman, and JFK be saying if they were alive?

The last two democratic presidents have cut military spending. In doing this, they had made it difficult for the military to do its job effectively. The democratic leadership, as it is now configured, consist of a great number of people that have grown up in the anti-war Vietnam era.

Other than Barak Obama, the majority of younger democrats in the congress are people that subscribe to the FDR/JFK theory of politics. Be liberal on social issues but be conservative on National Security. Maybe these will be the people who will be the ones to force the party away from not being a viable party for a generation. The American people want to feel safe. This safe feeling would allow them to argue and solve social issues.

Please Confirm
04/24/2008

We have seen the acrimony that comes out each time President Bush has tried to get federal judges confirmed. There have been times when Senator Harry Reid has promised to confirm judges and has lied.

It has, sometimes, taken months, and sometimes years to get judges confirmed during this president's administration. That is a very sad state of affairs because during the Clinton administration all of his judges were confirmed in a quick and timely fashion.

We will see if Harry Reid will make himself into a liar, AGAIN.

Religiosity
04/25/2008

It now appears that we have a religious state legislature in Louisiana. A great number of both houses appear to have more that an average belief if God.

The first place it is showing is in Ben Never's bill about creationism/intelligent design.

It also appears some lawmakers are having bible study meetings before the sessions tart in their respective chambers in the legislature.

Will this be a permanent thing? Will it be specific to this legilature? The answers to these questions are, let us wait and see.

Ugliness
04/27/2008

The democrat nominating process for the office of the president is getting real messy. They just keep hammering away at each other. As they continue, it makes it more unlikely they will combine forces to form the dream ticket the democrat higher-ups want.

The negative ads are flying. They are coming so fast that it is almost hard to keep up with

As much as I am lukewarm about the fact that John McCain is the republican nominee, he is still a better choice over the two democrats.

It has been said that this is the last shot for the boomers to mold and shape the country. If either McCain or Hillary Clinton wins, that will be the case. I am not sure what to think about Barak Obama.

The irony of this is that all the ugliness happening on the democratic side may actually help either of those candidates to win the presidency.

Campaign Ads.
04/29/2008

What might some campaign ads look like in the general elecion?

That is a very interesting question.

We all know there will definitely be some attack ads, that is a given. If there are some, shall we say, softer ads, then they will be few and far between.

Different ads will be run against different democratic opponents. There is a shot that if Hillary Clinton wins, there will not be a lot of negative ads against her. She has had very high (50%) unfavorable ratings. With Barak Obama, it will, not only be his policies, but it will also be his associations. His preacher, his friends, and the person who helped him buy his house will definately be the focus of negative ads.

Both democratic candidates have character flaws which will be easily be pointed out in these commercials.

Yes, John McCain has his own set of problems, but his problems are of the type that can be overcome.

Money Troubles
04/29/2008

John McCain could be in trouble. If he decides to take matching public campaign fund, he definately will be in trouble.

The problem stems from the fact that Barak Obama and Hillary Clinton can raise gobs of money from the internet and other less ethical places.

We know about the Clinton's and foreign money. It is, supposedly, illegal to accept money from foreign countries and foreing sources.

I am not saying that McCain should accept "dirty" money, but he has to do something to make up the monetary distance between himself and his democratic opponents.

Energy Bill, Energy Tax, or Government Hand-Out? by Jillian Bandes
04/30/08

The 648-page energy bill just penned by Democratic Reps. Henry Waxman and Edward Markey is ostensibly designed to reduce greenhouse gas emissions and save money. But conservatives contend that the bill is nothing more than a tax, adding costs to energy producers and distributors for unproven methods of greenhouse gas emissions. These costs would be passed on to consumers to the tune of $3,900 per year, per household.

To be sure, the cost of the bill is its most frightening aspect; however, there are a few other tricks in the bill that deserve some attention.

Rep. John Shadegg (R-Ariz.) highlighted the fact that this legislation would make it possible for any American to sue any other American on the grounds that he was being adversely affected by that person's pollution. If a plaintiff is a "victim of climate change," or even believes that becoming a victim is "at risk of occurring," he is eligible to sue.

Townhall.com searched for additional factoids in the bill, being debated this week in Congress:

Lobbying restrictions, p. 56: Corporations who are tied in well enough with Congressmen can feel free to lobby Congress for more regulations that will provide them with an advantage over their competitors.

Waivers, p. 70: Corporations the government deems worthy enough won't have to comply with the regulations in the bill.

Smart Grid analysis, p. 91: Analysis of the benefits of the so-called government "Smart Grid" will be done using an imagined scenario where citizens are using the "Smart Grid" to the best of their ability – with no actual specifications as to what is the "best of their ability."

Lamp shapes, p. 128: If a company wants Congress to certify that its lamp shapes are better than its competitor's lamp shapes, they should feel free to petition their Congressman.

Labeling, starting on p. 201: Over nine pages of instructions on how "green" products must be labeled.

Art work light fixtures, p. 226: Artists shouldn't even think about creating a piece of artwork involving light fixtures that fall outside the regulations outlined in this section of the bill.

City planning regulations, p. 277: Government can now regulate parking lots in individual communities.

Al Gore-style global warming scare tactics, p. 325: "Global warming and its adverse effects are now occurring and are likely to continue and in crease in magnitude, and to do so at a greater and more harmful rate, unless this Act is fully implemented and enforced in an expeditious manner." In other words, this Act will, in fact, save the world.

Mandatory review of global warming, p. 329: The liberal National Academies of Science has unilateral authority to make recommendations to Congress as the result of this bill.

Standards for Federal Greenhouse Gas Registry, p. 350: Government must seek the opinion of qualified liberal environmental groups when creating or revising the registry.

Regarding offset programs, p. 404: Special interest groups may petition to have their individual needs served by Congress.

Regarding aviation safety, p. 511: Cars can be regulated until the cows come home, but airplanes, which may be "greener" than cars, get a free pass because the industry has a higher profile.

Providing for workforce training and sustainable practices, p. 566: "Secretary shall award grants to institutions of higher education to provide workforce training and education in industries and practices….." This includes "sustainable culinary practices.")

We, all the time, talk about the bloated federal government. What is really bad is the bloated federal government putting forward bloated federal legislation.

What eventually happens is that they ultimately try to stuff a lot of things in to these bills that should not be there. It gets really bad when, particularly, the democrats are in power.

It is said by Rush Limbaugh,

"The democrats are funny when they are out of power, and dangerous when they are in power."

That is correct.

The republicans may be just a dangerous. That party should be more conservative as they are. Of course, I think that a lot of these republican people recall respect for Theodore Roosevelt. He was the early version of John McCain and the rhino-republicans.

The democrats current energy bill has a lot of things that should not be in it. We all understand that these people are beholden to the environmental lobby. That particular lobby is killing the country. They are so hard headed that they will not allow the all of the above theory of energy production. They despise the oil companies and drilling is a strict no-no. They, also, want nothing to do with Nuclear Energy. The fact that most of the European countries get a majority of their energy from it.

Back to the current energy bill put forward by the democrats.

Some of the things that will happen are:

1. There will be more lobbing not less.

2. There will be waivers handed out to the companies that they like.

3. There must be labeling that tells the danger of certain things (e.g. compact Florescent lightulb).

4. Rules on the shpe of your lampshade.

5. Artists can't paint or sculpt what you see.

6. Regulation of parking lots.

Those are just a few of the idiotic things that are in this bill.

Scary
05/01/2008

Louisiana can not afford to have Governor Bobby Jindal leave to become the vice president in the middle of his first term. All of the, so-called, reform that he has worked toward would be undone by Lieutenant-Governor Mitch Landrieu. Landrieu is a liberal democrat. He is also a part of the "Good Ole Boy" network.

Mitch Landrieu's sister, "Katrina" Mary Landrieu, is up for reelection for her office. If he is in office as the governor, it might it more likely his sister gets reelected and retains here office. He will also get to choose who his replacement for Lieutenant-Governor will be.

Why should a man who couldn't even beat the inept idiot Mayor Ray "Chocolate City" Nagin deserve to be the governor of the state of Louisiana.

That is truly a scary thought.

On The March
05/02/2008

It is generally considered this will be a a great year politically for the democrats. They are should make gains in both the house and the senate, and possibly win the White House. I do not subscribe to that conventional wisdom.

The feeling I get is there will be an unpopular president and a even more unpopular congress. The congress is not just unpopular but it is also ineffective. This could be one of those years that will split the government.

The republican need not forget Woody Jenkins. If they were to forget him it would hurt the nation. It appears they are not going to forget about him because the NRCC and republican groups are pouring just as much money into this election as the DCCC. They are making this election just as important as the one against the democratic incumbent Mary Landrieu.

These two seats that are being run for and the seats of retiring senators and representatives are very important; because, if the republicans can win them it could serve as a buffer against the democrats and their agenda.

The Day
05/03/2008

It is now upon us. Today is election day in Louisiana. Who will win, will it be Don Cazyaoux or Woody Jenkins?

Cazayoux is a democrat and says he is a conservative, blue-dog. Jenkins may very, well be the real conservative. I firmly believe there are now no conservative democrats. Cazayoux is trying to masquerade as a conservative. I think, even if Cazayoux is a conservative, and is elected, he will be called into the back rooms of democratic power and told, in now uncertain terms, that if he wants to get reelected he will have to vote down party lines.

Woody Jenkins, on the other hand is the true conservative. Yes, there are liberal to liberal-rhino republicans, but I don' think Jenkins is one of those. I think he does want to cut taxes and believe is the sanctity of human life. He also believes the war on terror exists and we need him to win.

We need him to get elected so that if the democrats get elected to power, it will be harder for them to get their policies enacted.

This election has gotten ugly. The democratic national committee has decided to do their usual hatchet job on the conservative candidate. I truly think that Woody Jenkins is a good, law-abiding person. But, through negative ads, he has been painted as otherwise. He has been attacked on character and not on policies. Whereas, I think Jenkins has attacked Cazayoux only on policy.

It was a genius move for Jenkins to try and link Cazyoux to Nancy Pelosi. By doing this, the republicans are trying to say that he will vote down party lines. They, also, are trying to link him to the lowest ranked (by poll) congress in the history of this great country.

I know who I want to win. Will the election come out that way? We won't know until late tonight.

Food Woes
05/05/2008

It now seems that because we are now mandating ethanol, it is a contributing factor in the rising price of food. We are telling farmers we need more corn for ethanol, leading to them planting less of everything else and planting more corn.

Crops like wheat, rye, barley, etc. are not being grown in large quantities. This means that foods made from these grains are going to go up in price. Look for foods like bread, cereal, beer and others made from these grains to have a higher price at the market.

I am not saying the people are going to go hungry. But, the fact that farmers will be growing mostly corn will directly lead to a decrease in some staple products used mostly in the diet of some poor people.

This may be an alarmist way of thinking, but the more we go in that direction the more chance we will have a food woe.

Sense And Nonsense.
05/06/5008

Sometime one can not wrap his are her brain around thing that the government (federal, state, or local) does.

A great example of that is the current gun debate. The law states that you can conceal and carry a gun in the state of Louisiana.

Why should it be illegal to carry a gun onto the campus of a college and university. The fact of the matter is that there should be no debate. This people that are making it an issue are the gun control people. These are the same persons that want to take away all guns. They also don't like how the U.S. Constitution reads and wish that they could easily change it.

That is why we are having this debate about a law that is supposedly written in stone.

In It Until The Bitter End
05/07/2008

Yesterday, there were two more primary battles for the democratic nomination for the presidency. What the people expected to happen actually occurred. There was a split. Hillary Clinton won in Indiana and Barak Obama won in North Carolina.

It now creates an assurance that Clinton will stay in the campaign through the convention. There is some pressure for her to get out, but it is not strong enough for it to matter to her at this time.

If they keep splitting wins, they WILL take this thing to the convention. If that happens and either/or gets the nomination, the theory is that the others voters will either stay at home or vote for John McCain.

Even though John McCain has his problems, he is an immanently better choice than either of the democratic choices.

It will be fun to watch the democratic convention. The infighting that will occur outside the convention could be amusing and interesting.

There could be a major riot.

In my mind, there is no chance there will be a reconciliation between those two democratic candidates. There has been too much acrimony.

The only option, as I see it, is for them to choose another candidate at the convention. By doing this, it will save the party form being ripped apart at the scenes.

There is a great amount of people who do not want to see Hilliary in the president's office. There is, also, an amount of racism that might not allow some democrats to vote for Obama.

All in all, this is making democracy fun to watch.

Get The Petrol
05/08/2008

Oil is now approaching $200 a barrel. As is does, the world gets bigger. What I mean, is that as the price of oil gets higher, it makes it less likely that one will travel. Our food prices will get higher. Don't even talk about the multitude of things that are produced from oil.

What are we doing?

Why are we not drilling in ANWR, off of the Gulf Coast, west coast, and in other places?

Why are we not making gas from coal?

Those are just a few questions that need to be answered.

What we need to do is to call in all of the environmentalist wack-o groups and tell them to go and take a flying leap. Those people are definitely hurting our country. Their beliefs are hurting national security. I fear none of the three presidential candidates will address this topic unless we, the people, force them to.

The more time goes by the more beholding we get to foreign oil.

It's Not Their Money
05/09/2008

The Buddy Shaw bill, alone, would have given hard working, middle-class families a much deserved tax cut.

It would have been one of the easiest things the state government could have done. Sometimes the government makes things harder then they should be.

This was a good case and point.

Governor Bobby Jindal wants any tax cut to be offset by a corresponding spending cut. It need not be that way because Jindel is the governor. He can change his mind and whatever bill that is put forward, can be passed. He is the most powerful governor in the country.

The bill that is attached to Shaw's bill was a state income tax cut. That, too, is a good idea. However, this issue should be treated as a separate issue. I would love to see a permanent repeal of the state income tax because it would give people the incentive to work.

The Shaw bill, on the other hand, would end up having the effect of helping the public out with their everyday living by putting money in their hands to assist them with expenses, such as high energy prices.

Our lawmakers, sometimes, can not see the forest through the trees. They try to make bills too good and in the process kill them. Whereas, if they would leave them alone, they would pass, get signed, and help the general public.

The second thing I do not understand is why the governor, who ran on lower taxes, would be against this bill? He is keeping quiet on the issue. Please, Governor Jindal, speak out and tell us, the people who elected you, why did you help to kill the Shaw bill? The public wants to know.

What To Do?
05/10/2008

The next president, whomever he or she may be, will face a test from Iran within the first hundred days of the new administration. That is my prediction.

What will the new president do, and how will the challenge be faced?

My idea is, if it is a challenge on the seas, to tell the captain of USS Joe Blow to have a no tolerance policy. This means if the Iranian vessel comes across in anything close to a threatening manner, the captain is to give the order to blow it out of the water. The message this will send is to tell the Iranians that this new president does not play. It will also put the fear of God in them in the same manner President Ronald Reagan did when he told Mohmar Qaddafi, "The bmbing begins at dawn."

If this is done, Iran WILL NOT want to roll around with America.

When Is It Too Much?
05/12/2008

There may very well be too much media coverage of this years presidential election. Then maybe there is a case to be made that the coverage is just enough.

The fact of the matter is when a candidate is pretending to be something he or she is not, it is the media's job to investigate to prove the candidate is less than truthful.

In the case of Barak Obama, he is a person that the general public knew very little about. The public knew nothing about Jeremiah Wright. Wright is the controversial preacher that may help to cost the democrats the White House. Then, there is Bill Ayers. This is the unrepentant terrorist that bombed governmental installations. The man has said that he should have bombed even more. What about Tony Rezko? He may have ties to organized crime.

If it weren't for the new media, the associations to Obama would not be coming out.

There is supposed to be a full examination of the candidates when they are running to be the "Leader of the Free World."

I think that the media coverage in this year's presidential election has brought to light some interesting facts about our candidates, especially the democrats.

Wrong
05/13/2008

There are speculations that the GOP has permanently lost, in a special election, the sixth congressional seat in a special election in the state of Louisiana. Dan Cazyoux, a democrat appears to be the winner.

I firmly disagree.

I, sincerely, think the seat can be won back by the GOP again. The fact is that the way politics works, anybody of any party can win any seat he wants as long as he has the money or can get the money from the state and national GOP.

The state GOP needs to get off of their behinds and do their jobs so that they can win back that seat. They also need to have the guts to use his voting record, which he will have when the November election comes.

Greatest Hour
05/14/2008

A majority of the punditry is predicting a great defeat for the GOP.

I firmly disagree. This could be the conservative movements greatest hour.

There are people that are running, on the democrat side of the isle, as conservatives. Rush Limbaugh has just said it, "If Nancy Pelosi has to, she will run conservative democrats to help her have a super majority."

That is a good and a bad move. It is a good move because it will, possibly, give her a super majority. It is a bad move because some of the potential electees are independent thinkers. Case and point, Dan Cazyoux. She better make sure they are on the same page. If they are not, there could be a deep fissure in the democratic party.

If what I think will happen does happen, we will see those so-called "conservative" democrats suddenly lurch to the left.

Who Will They Pick?
05/15/2008

We, in Louisiana, have several democratic congressional members.

I bet you did not know there is an election going on?

I really don't care who the Louisiana democratic contingent endorses. Both the democratic choices are bad for the country. I am not saying John McCain is any better, but I do know, for sure, that I will not vote for either of the democrats. I may very well be voting for "none-of-the-above."

It seems to be most of the candidates from the two major political parties are almost the same person. The only difference is McCain is much stronger on national defense.

Leaders And Followers
05/16/2008

There are politicians of many stripes. There are crooks and liars. There are, also, ones with good character. There are competent and incompetent ones. Whomever the people get, the most important quality to possess is that he be a leader and not a follower.

The problem is sometimes the people elect a person they think is a leader but which, on certain issues, end up having to be led around by the nose by the people.

I like Governor Bobby Jindal. I voted for him. But in the case of the Stelley Bill, the people had to lead him around by the nose. We can also say the same thing about the majority of the legislature. These lawmakers were elected to help lead the state out of the doldrums and into a new day. When they do not get out in front of the issue, they seemed to want to keep the status quo. For whatever reason, they did not seem to want to get rid of the bad bill. The people wanted the Stelley Bill gone and they "got it gone".

All of these new lawmakers got into office by promising to change things. When they promise to make changes and do not get to the front of these changes, the people will do the right thing and get rid of them. We want leaders and not followers.

Will The Conservatives Take Back The GOP?
05/17/2008

There is a line in a country song, "You have got to stand for something or you will fall for anything." If this does not describe the GOP at both the state and federal level, then, I don't know what does.

The GOP, it seems, has lost its way. It has morphed into a high spending party. It has, also, morphed into a more liberal party. To quote Vince Lombardi "what the hell is going on here."

If things keep going the way they are, the democrats may win the White House and will have a super majority in both the house and the senate. That is definitely a scary proposition.

If this happen one might see higher taxes, despite a presidential veto. It may, also, lead to more bad environmental legislation. This legislation will definitely hurt the country. It will hurt, because fuel has gotten to be a national security issue. The less we have because of us not going in and drilling, the more we have to depend on outside sources from foreign countries; who may not necessarily be our friends.

The GOP needs to reconstitute itself. It may take McCain getting blown out for the party to do it. If they don't do it, there may be another forty years of a democratic congress.

Shaping
05/19/2008

From the time of the Greeks and the Romans through this current time, democracy has shaped the world. If the autocrats, terrorists, and democrats have their way, then fanaticism and autocracy will shape the next.

The democrats want to pull out of Iraq. They want to capitulate with and negotiate with Iran and North Korea. They love people like Raul Castro and the leader of Argentina. Of course, liberals have had this mindset for many years. They wanted to keep slavery. When that did not happen, they consistently voted for racist laws to keep the black-Americans down. They appeased Hitler. Here in the United States, since World War II, any time a president wanted to do the right thing and fight evil and injustice, they stood in the way. From Vietnam through Granada and the Philippines and now with Iraq, they are at it again.

These liberal democrats are trying to shape the world in a peacenik way. That has been proven over and over not to work. Only in a few cases has it been successful. Ganhdi and Nelson Mandela have both been men of great character and strong wills, and have made it work. I don' think the liberal side of the isle has leaders that are of their statute. The democratic leaders are persons of the sixties, or have be influenced and shaped by radical agendas.

The current crop of democrat leaders have been shaped by people like Ted Kennedy. What needs to happen is for some of the younger democrats to step up and change their party and give it another direction.

Enablers
05/20/2008

The west is enabling terror. Take a look at Hesbollah. The west's leaders say they want to defeat terror and wipe it out. The problem is the west is not treating Hezbollah the same as they treat all other terrorists.

Hesbollah is the proxy of a proxy. They are the group that is directly funded by Syria; and, supported by Iran.

The main problem is that Hezbollah has worked itself into the leadership of the government of the West Bank, and is trying to to do the same is Lebanon.

The west simply can not allow this to happen. The problem is that we do not have the grapefruit to do this. We could eradicate them as easily as we change socks, but we seem only to just want to talk to them.

State Of The Political Parties
05/21/2008

The state of both of the major political parties in this nation is poor.

On the one side, the democrats lean so far to the left they are are out of the mainstream of American society. They have lost their way from great past leaders of their parties. Presidents like Andrew Jackson, Franklin D.Roosevelt, Harry Truman, and John F.Kennedy were closer to the people than this current crop of democrats. The republicans aren't any better. They have morphed into democratic party lite. They have gotten away from wanting to cut taxes and spending. There are even republicans who believe in the hoax of global warming.

The fact of the matter is both of the parties have big problems. Democrats are too diverse and republicans are inept. Democrats want to pit one group of people against another, while republicans don't know how to defend themselves from the attacks that come from the other side.

That makes for a sad state of political affairs in this nation.

Who To Negotiate With
05/22/2008

There are certain people that you negotiate with and certain persons that you don't.

The reason you don't negotiate with certain parties is if they promise something, that promise will not be worth anything.

I have a feeling that Iran falls into that situation. They have been belligerent and have refused to do what they have been ordered to do by the world leaders to maintain peace. The Mullahs and Adminadijihad refuse to stop working toward nuclear weapons. They need to be taught a lesson. The problem we are facing is that there are some in this country's leadership that don't want this to happen. We, also, know who these people are. They are the people who came of age during the 1960's

These people want another Jimmy Carter. Carter was a huge mistake as a president. It was so bad during his time in office, that there was a misery index. There was high inflation, and he led directly to the current situation with Iran.

That is how bad of a president Barak Obama would make. He will be just like Carter.

Getting Better
05/23/2008

What can the GOP do to get better?

It needs to return to its roots of Lincolnism and Reaganism. As of this date, the GOP is known for big spending and "off the field" scandals. They need to get back to what they do best.

There is a definite difference how the democrat's big money supporters and the GOP's big money supporters donates to their respective parties. There is George Soros, who has a endless supply of money at the disposal of the democratic party. Then there is the democratic attakc blogs like the Huffington Post. The combination of those two entities is a concerted effort the GOP has yet to figure out how to combat.

Even though the current president has figured out ways in which to politically outflank the donkeys, the rest of the party has yet to pick that ball up and run with it.

In short, the republican party needs to step up and lead. As it stands at this point in time, there is no one in the national republican party wishing to do that. It will take someone like Bobby Jindal to do that.

Having Issues
05/24/2008

President George W. Bush may say that the comments about Iran and Iraq he made at the Knesset was not sent out to any particular candidate. Who is he fooling. Both of the democratic candidates for the office in which he currently resides have said they want to withdraw troops as soon as possible. Don't even talk about what the majority of the lily-livered, democrat-led congress said they want to do.

President Bush made the right comments at that time. The facts are if we were to withdraw too soon, all of the progress that has been made would be in vain. That mistake would be on the same vain as the one made by President G.H.W. Bush in not going to Baghdad and removing Saddam Hussein. It would weaken the national government. The other thing that it would do is to take whatever love and good will the Iraqi people have for the United States and flush it down the drain.

The two democratic presidential candidates come from a congress that is the worst rated congress in the history of the country. The president has low ratings, but the congress is lower. If they wanted to end the war they could cut the funding. The House of Representatives holds the purse strings. They don' dare do that because they are afraid of the blowback that would come from the American people. I have said it before, the American people like to win. If the government takes that away, then what?

The democrats are afraid if they do what the kooks of their party want, it will set their party back for generations. It would not matter who they get to run, they could not run on national security.

The Rule
05/26/2008

The congress has voted or will vote on the current FCC rule about media ownership. This is about cross ownership. As it stands right now, a company can own a newspaper, televison, and radio station in the same market. I don't see the problem with that.

The argument is diversity. The problem is it takes a great deal of money to own one of the three types of media. It takes a lot of money to publish a news paper. It take a great deal of money to own and run a television staton. The cheapest thing is a radio station. If you have between four and fifteen thousand dollars, you can start a low power FM radio station.

The congress needs to let the market figure out and decide what it wants to do. If the market, in any city in the country, wants to allow one person or company to own all three parts of the major media, then so be it.

Reaganism Is Dying
05/27/2008

A movement was born in 1976. It was born of a man with strong beliefs and high moral character. Ronald Reagan believed in low taxes, a strong national defense, and small government. I wish that there were more republicans like him.

Conservatism seems to be withering on the vine. The size of government has grown. It also seems there are more and more entitlements. The fact of the matter is that republicanism has become as dirty of a word as liberal.

It will take someone of high moral character to come in and to take the party back. There is a rebuilding job that needs to be done. It is a very big undertaking. It will be up to the younger republicans to do this because the older ones are of the John McCain ilk.

We need republicans that grew up in the 1980's. Those people will understand Reagan and his ways.

Beginning Of Reform Presidencies
05/28/2008

Everyone knows there are more than enough things about the federal government that need to be reformed. Both of the democratic presidential candidates claim they are the reform candidate. I don't know if I can believe any of them.

John McCain can be the beginnings of reform. This will be a tough, long process that will probably stretch possibly two terms of his presidency and the presidencies of multiple other lawmakers. The fact of the matter is that it might be extremely hard to get the ball rolling with an extremely democratic congress. Some of the thing that he might propose would be little too conservative for them.

Things like reform of the Social Security system will be exceedingly tough because some of the lawmakers are a little stubborn. They think the current system is good enough and will last forever.

Don't even talk about anything military, because on that side of the isle, the older democrats hate and loathe the armed forces. The last two democratic presidents have made major cuts to the Pentagon.

Any tax reform might be a non starter. Democrats like high tax rates. They are into redistribution of wealth in a big way. They consider themselves to be like Robin Hood. McCain needs to take back Robin Hood and make him what he was in the first place, a conservative. He needs to explain that it was not the rich that Robin Hood was stealing from, but it was the high taxes that was oppressing the people. The high taxes led to some of the English having their lands taken by the government.

Again, it will be a daunting job for McCain to do. Does he have the energy to get the ball rolling downhill?

Rethink Themselves
05/29/2008

It is time for the feminist movement to rethink itself. As it stands right now, this movement is just another constituent of the democratic party.

It was once a strong movement. It is no longer. Hillary Clinton has done a great deal to weaken its power. The fact of the matter is, by her standing by her man, Bill, throughout the whole Monica incident and the many other sexual alliances he has had, she has weakend the movement for her political success.

The quietness of this movement on the mistreatment of Moslem women is defining. If this movement was worth its salt, it would be speaking up loudly for the rights of those women. In this respect, it has fallen down on the job.

The biggest surprise is that women's rights is for abortion. Childbirth is one of the most sacred thing about a woman. Men can make no claim to what a woman goes through in childbirth. If is often said men could not handle the pain.

If things do not change, the movement will die and the power it has gained for women will be largely forgotten.

His Time Will Come
05/30/2008

Bobby Jindal is a rising star in the republican party. Even though he has some minor missteps, he is still well-liked.

We understand that John McCain is looking for a conservative to counterbalance the belief that he is a little bit too liberal. McCain may consider Jindal for the vice president's position but Louisiana needs him more than McCain does.

The current lieutenant governor is from the Louisiana democratic machine. Mitch Landreiu is a very liberal democrat. If he were to be in office at this time, who knows what kind of damage he could do. One thing that might happen is that his sister's congressional seat, which a lot of the pundits deem as being in serious trouble of being lost to republicans, might possibly end up staying in the democrats hands. That would be a sad turn of events; because, she is a yes vote for a lot of the liberal agendas Nancy Pelosi, Harry Reid, and possibly Barak Obama are going to try to get passed.

The fact is that Jindal still has some work to do so that he can build up his credentials to become a legitimate presidential candidate. This means not only do we need him to stay, but it would behoove him to stay so that he would be the republican that would possibly follow what would be potentially be one of the worst presidencies in the history of the United States. Barak Obama is a good candidate but will be, in my opinion, a poor president. His time in office could be every bit as bad as Jimmy Carter's.

Jindal's time will come, but it is not now.

What Now?
05/31/2008

Thanks to a combination of governmental entities (state and national) and non-governmental entities (environmental groups), we have not been able to get the oil that is rightfully ours. It is largely these two groups that have led to the raising of the prices that caused the people to give up necessities.

Because of the fact people have cars and use them, they need to have fuel to run them. Because fuel alternatives are cost prohibitive, this means it cost the same or less than drilling for and refining petrol, oil is the way to go. We need to get as much of it as possible. Another fact is, the general public would rather run their cars on petroleum based derivatives.

We need to be allowed to go out there and to get what is rightfully ours.

By attacking the oil companies, they are, in essence and reality, attacking the general public. Most of the stocks of oil companies are owned by the general public. With high taxes and oppressive environmental laws, the government has essentially hurt regular people.

The government's attitudes need to change.

He Quit
06/01/2008

Barak Obama has quit Trinity United Church. There have been so many controversial comments for the pulpit of that church, it made it more than a certainty he would have to resign his membership.

What we are not sure of is whether or not Obama actually believes what was spouted from that pulpit. If he does, then this could be a scary thought. I can't see how he has not been influenced by the teachings of this church, because he was a member of that congregation for twenty years. He, also, married a very radical woman, whom I think, also, believes what was being preached there.

A lot of the so-called pundits believe that these things will not hurt Obama. I firmly disagree. You only have to look at what occurred in the democratic primaries of Ohio and West Virginia. Ohio happened after the first time Jeremiah Wright made his comments. Obama lost big. West Virginia took place following the comments of Wright and the new pastor at Trinity. Again, he got dominated.

Will his past alliances hurt him in the general election? I hope so because I don't think that America can stand a president that is just left of Stalin.

Recoverable
06/02/2008

A United States Bureau of Land Management report states that, there are forty-one billion barrels of oil and two-hundred-thirty-one trillion cubic feet of natural gas located on onshore lands.

There are several impediments that have "environmental" concerns. We all know there are groups of "wack-os" that don't want us to develop any potential places, onshore or offshore, that might help us to alleviate our supply and demand problems. There is, also, the antiquities act, passed long ago when oil supplies were down, that have surpressed oil drilling. There are several "National Parks" that have been created, that should not have been. On these park's land is where the majority of this oil and natural gas is located.

These "Environmentalist" groups don't want to drill anywhere.

We need this oil to help us at the pump. It may only be a three month supply, but every little bit helps.

Veeps
06/03/2008

It look like both of the presumptive nominees for the office of the President of the United States has been chosen. Now comes the important choices for both candidates. Who will be their respective Vice Presidents running mates.

For John McCain, he needs to have a rock solid conservative. For Barak Obama, since he is considered to be an elitist, his choice needs to appeal to hard-working, blue-collar Reagan democrats.

It does not matter if McCain and Romney went at each other. Romney should be the choice. There are others on the, so called, list for the job, but the majority of them are young and probably not ready for an important responsibility this office presents. McCain is not a "spring chicken". In fact, his father died of a heart attack in his mid-seventies and McCain is already seventy-two.

In Obama's case, he is a young man without a lot of real-world and political experience. His choice needs to be a person with a lot of multi type experiences. Jim Webb fits the bill. The man was in Vietnam, so he has the same foreign policy experience as McCain. Unlike Obama, he has author some bills that have gotten through. Most importantly, he appeals to the same democrats that Hilliary Clinton appeals to.

Those should be the respective choices for the respective presumptive candidates.

All Thing Aren't Equal
06/04/2008

There are some problems with Louisiana's Governor Bobby Jindal and there are things he is doing right. He refuse to give the people tax relief from the Stelley Bill. He has not allowed some of the largest amount of funding that has, in the past, been sent to home districts to not "go home."

That is a good thing. A lot of things that have went out to certain districts have not been needed and were big wastes of the taxpayers money. This pork needed to be gutted out of the bloated state budget and it appears it has been.

Jefferson Parish is griping about not getting its "fair share" of the port in the capital outlay bill. The more they complain, the more they look greedy. They wanted money to expand the Huey

P. Long Expressway. There is, also, the money that would fix other roads in the area. Then, there is the hospital-financing bill that would have given money back to public hospital for treating uninsured patients.

That was definitely pork and needed to be cut out.

We need the governor to be more consistently conservative on a lot more of the issues. If he is not, then, he is no better then most of the politicians that we have had throughout the history of this state.

Get The Oil
06/05/2008

There is enough oil in the ground in this great country to get us off of foreign sources today. The democrats continue to keep voting down bills that will not allow us to drill for this oil. That is a sad state of affairs.

Over and over again, they keep voting to hurt the country. By voting this way, they keep hurting the economy. This country survives by truck. Everything that is fit to ship gets there by truck. Trucks run on diesel fuel. The higher the price of diesel, the higher the price of the products that get shipped. The price of food is going up along with the price of gas. They are "getting" the "real" Americans, coming and going.

The combination of higher prices and our lack of ability of getting our own sources of domestic sources of oil will bring us to our knees.

If we could get our own sources of oil, it would be a stopgap so that we could develop "new technologies." This is what the democrats say they want. However, some of these "new technologies" are cost prohibitive. This means that only the rich can afford to buy the cars that operate on them. The free market needs time to drive the prices of these "new technologies" down so all American citizens can afford to buy them.

This is one of the reasons for congress' popularity rating being in the tank. The more the democratic party allows itself to be ruled by the environmental lobby, the more the American general public will continue to be hurt.

Accouterments
06/06/2008

We not ony need to get the oil, but we need to get all of the accouterments that go along with it. This definitely includes building more refineries.

Even if we did go out and drill for, and found some oil, the current refining capacity would only allow for the exact amount of oil to get refined that we currently have in existence.

We need to build more refineries. Every other country is doing this. If we don't, we are stupid.

The facts are that the democrats, the mainstream press, and their willing accomplices in the "environmental" movement are standing in the way. They are destroying the greatness of America.

Oil is what runs the engine of freedom. We, not only, run our vehicles on it, but we, also, make other products from it. The odds are you may be wearing something that, in some part, was made from oil. We write with it. It helps to preserve the food we eat. There are many more uses of oil originated products use by the American people every day.

If we don't do every thing it takes to get the oil, it could bring us to our knees.

At What Cost? Equality
06/07/2008

It now appears New York state will recognize same-sex unions from other states.

The same-sex marriage community is happy about this decision. They see it as the first step to New York state accepting same-sex marriages.

If you examine this topic closely, the states that recognize gay marriage and the ones that accept them are all liberal states. They are the ones that are willing to be beholden to liberal interest groups. They are, also, the most non-religious states.

The fact is God can't be wrong. He said that being homosexual is wrong. He also made it clear that marriage is to be between a man and a woman. What these "liberal" states and countries are saying is that God is wrong, when in reality they are wrong.

Most gay folks just want to live their lives and to be left alone. They really don't care whether they are considered to be married or not. They are like most Americans, they are non-political.

The leadership of the lawmakers, on this subject, is the reason "God-fearing" people are leaving New York state in droves.

Gore Is A Chicken
06/09/2008

Recently, the Czeck president, Yaclav Klaus challenged Al Gore to a debate on the subject of global warming. Gore has yet to agree to the debate because there is a good shot he would get his "clock cleaned".

Yaclav Klaus is not only the President of the Czeck Republic but he is also an economist. This man is intelligent enough to know that this global warning hoax/religion would be a burden on any country's economy.

Gore thinks he is very smart. I tend to lean to the other side of this equation. I think that any preeminent thinker on global warming would want to prove how smart he is on this subject. Gore indicates he does not want to do this.

Where Is The Feminist Movement
06/10/2008

The feminist movement in the United States has been a strong movement over the last half century. The women of this country have gotten a lot of advancements in women's rights.

The have gotten the right to vote. They have gotten the right to work. They have gotten the right to earn equal pay. They are now doing jobs that were traditionally set aside only for men.

There are problems with the feminist movement. One of their stated goals, when they first started, was the protection of women from mistreatment. They have not done that.

The facts are there.

The latest example of this is what is going on in Iran.

There is a group of women in Iran that are fighting for equal rights. They are trying to get 1000 signatures so that they can get something done. The "Islamic Republic" leadership does not want this to happen. They have begun to put these women into prison.

Where are the rest of the worlds feminists? They should be out spoken in support of their sisters in Iran.

They are falling down on their job.

Young Talent
06/11/2008

In the world of politics there are some young and talented folks. The talent does not just within the democrats and republicans, but many are nonpartisan.

The majority of these people are between the ages of 24 and 35. They are the "young guards" for all sides of politics.

These are the people who are helping to get the young, up-coming politicians elected to high offices. Without them, there would not be turnover from the old stale leadership, on both sides of the isle, to the new people who have fresh ideas to turn the country around.

In the republican camp, Melissa Sellers in Louisiana, helped to get Bobby Jindal, a potential future presidential candidate, elected to the governor's office; not been held by a person of color in its history. Justine Lam helped Ron Paul to raise a record amount of money online in Paul's quest for the president's office. Jessica Keegan is into the online media. David All is another fund raiser for the GOP. Luke Bernstein helped to get republicans elected in Pensylvania.

Will The Democrats Win The Presidency?
06/12/2008

The democrats think they will hold all of the power. They think it will turn out that their party will hold both the congress and the presidency. I think that they could be wrong.

Barak Obama's credentials are thin. He has not sponsored any major legislation. McCain, on the other hand, has been in the senate and has sponsored many bills, though they are a "mixed bag".

The American people don't know much about Obama. The man is still, very much, a blank slate. He has only been in the congress one-half of one term. That is not enough time for the American people to make a decision about you.

He is, also, coming from the democratic led congress that has the worst popularity rating in the history of the of the country.

We may get a "republican" in the White House and another democratic congress.

Vouchers In Small Towns
06/13/2008

If vouchers/school choice were enacted, how would it affect education in the small towns of Louisiana?

What probably would happen is the people who would use them would send their children to the local private or parochial school. It could also mean the more adventurous parents might try to home school their children.

These types of educational directions have the support of people from all classes, races, and social backgrounds of the state.

The most recent proposals that has come down the pipe has come from black democrats, Representative Austin Badon and Senator Ann Duplesis. Both of these legislators are from the poorest parts of the sate and, probably, graduated from inner-city schools. They are special cases because they seem to be high achievers.

We all know who the people opposing these types of laws which would be beneficial to a great number of lower income parents of the state. It is the teachers unions. That is a sad fact.

Do Ten Meetings
06/14/2008

Both Barak Obama and John McCain want to do joint town hall meetings. They have both agreed that they want to be able to have these meetings broadcast on multiple channels.

Michael Bloomberg and ABC news want these meetings to be exclusive to ABC.

I can see it from both points of view. ABC wants it exclusive because of the money. McCain and Obama want it on as many places as possible; so that as many people as possible will see these meetings.

ABC is looking to corner the market while the two candidates are looking to attract as many voters as possible.

The good thing about these town hall meetings are that they are not as formal as debates. They are not as rigid because they are not specifically run by the media. What is, also good about town hall meetings is that the candidates are open having questions not selected for them; therefore, not knowing what is coming next. The American people will actually be able to get their hands on the microphones and keyboards and not have their questions screened.

That is the way the process should be. The tough questions must be asked. It is up to the candidates to answer them in a straightforward fashion. If they don't, the public will not trust them, and see them for who the are. The ultimate goal is for the voters to see the candidates in action.

Google-ing A Veep
06/16/2008

John McCain has stepped into the twenty-first century. He is using Google to select his vice president running mate. He says it is much easier this way.

By doing it this way, it will allow him to concentrate on the democratic attacks that will surely come. He needs to have his mind on those attacks, so he can concentrate on the low–down dirty tricks the democrats will pull in order to win total and complete power.

Look for his veep candidate not to come from the list of, so-called, favorites. The man or woman that he chooses will be a dark horse in many of the pundits minds. The candidate will be conservative and at least twenty years younger than McCain.

I am not sure of an exact name, but whomever it is will be a person who will have the credentials to be in that job.

Boondoggle Stopped
06/17/2008

Recently, the current attempt of "fighting" global warming got held up. This bill was a good example of a "Christmas Tree" bill. It had so many bad amendments on it that it killed itself. It, also, got help because Senator Harry Reid would not allow some judicial appointments to come before the senate.

This bill was, and is, so bad, it would have hurt the country. It would have killed the economy. The people that are having trouble running their cars and warming and cooling their homes would have to make tremendous sacrifices. It would have killed the automotive aspect of the economy.

The fact is that it was the wrong bill at the wrong time.

The American people continue to be disappointed. The grassroots want to go out and get the oil, while the liberal democrats place roadblocks. Reverend Perry Stone has predicted there will be a serious backlash against the environmentlist "wack-o's". These lawmakers, who are blocking progress, should be voted out of office.

As We Win In Iraq, Prime Minister Al-Maliki Gets More Confiden
06/19/2008

As it gets more obvious that we are winning in Iraq, it is giving the Iraqi national government, lead by Nouri Al-Maliki, more confidence and power.

This leader is showing the initiative some of our politicians should have. There have been times, on the military side, things have been planned and he has jumped the gun and forced the plans to go sooner than they should have. It turns out, in most cases, he was right in doing what he did. Al-Qaeda in Iraq is all but defeated, and now they are working on defeating the Iranian backed Shiite militias.

The military successes are leading to political successes. They have figured out how to amicably split the oil revenues. There has been a bringing into the government the previously disgruntled Bathists; along with the rest of Sunni Iraq. The military winning has led to the ability of provisional and local governments to be able to be formed.

With all of the positive news coming out of Iraq, why do the democrats want to get out before the job is finished? It brings up what has been stated many times before. "What is good for America is bad for the democrats, and visa-versa."

Need To Change
06/20/2008

Obama's rhetoric needs to change. If he keeps saying what he is going to do, and does what he says he is going to do, it will cause irrepairable damage to the Iraq situation and to the coalition of the willing countries that are in the immediate area.

The military situation has definitely gotten better in Iraq. The actual battle for that country has swung in the favor of the United States and the Iraqi protection forces. The government is another success story. It has been able to pass laws that are making the lives of the Iraqi general public better. They have been able to bring in the ethnic groups of Iraq into the governance of the country.

If Obama does not tone down his rhetoric, all the gains that has been made might possibly go away. He needs to break form the far left of his party. If he does not, he will lose the election, big-time. There are national security democrats that will not vote for him. Even though the democratic party may very well win the congress, they could lose the White House in a big way.

Campus Protection
06/21/2008

Because there was a shooting on the campus of Virginia Tech University, there is strong consideration for the ability of the students and faculty to have gun permits for concealed weapons on university campuses.

In the great state of Louisiana an ex-parish sheriff is the one that is pushing the bill to allow this to happen.

The rationale behind this thought could have some merit. If an evil person on campus begins to shoot at others, a responsible person, trained in the usage of a weapon, could stop the amount of damage. In essence, it could save lives.

There are the usual persons and groups that are opposing this. They are mostly liberal and are gun control nuts.

It is thought that not a great number of people would get permits and carry guns. But, the ones who would could give our country added peace protection. Thes people could strengthen the constitutional rights to bare arms, that appears to be eroding due to the anti-gun lobby.

Starved
06/22/2008

According to the Battleground Poll's internal polling data, America is a majority conservative country. This should not bode well for the democrats; but, then, they have lied, cheated, and stolen their way to where the current elections have been made close.

The democratic lies begin by running, so-called, "conservative" democrats. They, also, have done a marvelous job of covering up their true feelings and thoughts on issues. They have made it, with the help of the press and the republicans, look like there is no difference between the parties. On issues like global warming, they have "jerry-rigged" things in such a fashion that they have skewed things in favor of the results they want. That is why so many of the last handful of election have appeared to be close.

If the republicans would just go back to their conservative roots, these elections might not be so close. There is a possibility that the punditry might, at any specific time, not say this would be a strong democratic year.

Character Builder
06/23/2008

We All know John McCain spent several years as a POW in the Hanoi Hilton. Hanoi Hilton was a brutal prisoner of war camp in Vietnam. It was, definitely, a character building time for John McCain.

The democrats may be running an uphill battle against McCain if they decide to run against his character. This man went into that camp and show the strength of character that is reserved for a very few people. I don't know if there is any of the current democrats that could have survived what McCain went through. They talk about the "torture" down at "Club GitMO", but they don't understand torture. McCain would have gladly traded Hanoi Hilton for a place like Guantanamo Bay.

The democrats have a habit of having selective amnesia. They remember only their party being responsible for stopping the Vietnam war. They forget that the war was on the way to being won when Watergate happened. If Nixon had not gotten stupid, the Vietnam war WOULD have been won.

It has been said that McCain has a bit of a temper. It takes a bit of a temper and some serious attitude to even think about being president of the United States. Our country, can not afford to forget about the Vietnam war. Forgetting about that war does the veterans, including John McCain, a great disservice.

True Silliness
06/24/2008

This hoax that is global warming is pure bilge. Let's grant that global warming is happening. It can be explained by scientists as a natural cycle of the earth.

The earth is a mighty and wonderful thing. It is bigger than the human race and, therefore, can not be affected by humanity.

As the sun goes, so goes the earth. If the sun puts out a lot of heat, the earth will be warmer. If there is an ebb in the amount of sunspots, the earth is going into a cooling cycle.

We have to ask ourselves just how can a substance like petroleum, that occurs naturally, hurt the earth? Most scientist maintain that it can not. If God did not want us to have it, He would not have put it in places where we could find it as easily as we can. Another thing is that it seems the more of it we use, the more of it we find.

If not for the $4.00 gas prices, that affects everything in our lives, this global warming would be relegated to the land of parody and jokes. There would be many skits on Saturday Night Live and Mad TV. It would border on beint ludicrous.

Supreme Battle
06/25/2008

The recent ruling of the Supreme Court about the Guantanamo detainees is another reason why the Supreme Court will remain a political issue.

The fact is, if Barak Obama wins the office of the presidency and win a majority in the congress, you can look for the older liberal justices to retire. They will decide this will be the right time to get a younger liberal replacement justice.

John McCain needs to win this election so we can continue to try to replenish the Supreme Court with conservative justices. As we keep doing this, there will be fewer liberal decisions coming down from the higher court.

Hot Air In Baton Rouge
06/26/2008

These are the "dog days of summer." This means this is the hottest most humid part of the summer. In past years, at this time of the year, there was very little exciting issues to talk about on talk radio.

This year is certainly not the case.

Usually the hot air coming out of the legislature at this time of the year amounts to nothing. This time of the year has given us such stupid ideas like a new state song or a state poem. Not this year, though. This time the lawmakers gave us a serious issue that the people could sink their teeth into. This issue is of legislative pay raises. It is no doubt the legislature has gotten greedy and a little to big for its britches. Should a child try to do the same thing these lawmakers are attempting to do, their parents would discipline them. As of now, the people are the disciplinarians. The people are extremely angry their legislator has voted themselves a massive pay raise. Our governor should veto this pay raise.

The legislators are insistant on voting themselves this pay raise and are defending their action. They are being insipid and childish on this issue. We are seeing many people trying to get their legislators recalled. That is the ultimate recourse. There are still others that are organizing marches on the legislature and the governor in the capital city.

The tide of the people is, in a major way, against the politicians. They are about to be smacked down in a major way. This is how a democracy is supposed to work.

Fake Republican With Genuine Praise
06/27/2008

Speaker of the house Jim Tucker is a person that gives slime a bad name. We know he is not a republican. What we did not know is that he would lie and try to intimidate people to his way of thinking. He is no more than a feckless thug.

This is a man who fought for these idiotic pay raises and who defends them. He is a man that helped Ann Duplesis pass a bill that has given the greedy legislature the money they do not deserve. Duplesis claims she needs more salary while she drives around in a Mercedes Benz SUV. Most poor people of our state have no vehicle.

Jim Tucker was brazenly arrogant when he got it passed and then he has attempted to intimidated the governor. We are now seeing the people trying to recall him. This has caused him to back off some of his threats. How shallow a character can a man have?

He is just one of a long list of legislators that need to go.

Who Do You Trust
06/28/2008

Taxes are some of the most hated things we know of. They hurt just about everyone.

It is obvious that Barak Obama and John McCain have diametrically opposing views on the subject. Obama is your classic tax and spend progressive liberal democrat, while McCain believes in low taxes for everyone.

The way the tax codes is set up, one needs to have a slide-rule to understand it. Our tax laws are so confusing. There are so many "ins and outs" it takes a person a couple of weeks even to understand the forms.

What would be fair, in terms of the amount we should pay, is the ten percent rule. God asks a person for only ten percent of his pay. Our government is asking for thirty-five percent. I understand that Jesus said "Render to God what belongs to God, and to Caesar what belongs to Caesar," but this does not mean that the government should be as greedy as it is.

You have to ask yourself the question, "Who do I trust the most to lower my taxes?"

It should be McCain.

Offshore
06/29/2008

John McCain now favors the repeal of the moratorium on offshore oil drilling that has existed since 1981.

I definitely agree with Senator McCain that it is time for this moratorium to be lifted. The high cost of oil by the barrel and gas/diesel at the pump demands it; as does the voices of the American voters.

There are environmental groups who don't understand their policies are hurting the country. The less we drill for our own oil, the more it hurts the blue collar, hard working American citizen. We simply can not afford to have these types of policies put animals, obviously not in any trouble, ahead of our national security.

The Chinese are going to help the Cubans drill off the coast of Florida. The American people SHOULD be concerned because that oil should be our oil.

Why are some republicans against drilling? These republican are referred to as "rhinos".

What I don't understand is when the polls say the American people are overwhelmingly in favor of drilling, why don't the weasel politicians do what the people want?

I think this is an issue that could be as big on the national stage as the legislative pay raises are on the state stage in Louisiana. This issue could be a tipping point for the public, metaphorically speaking, showing up with pitchforks and torches to try to kill the political Frankenstein monster, that is the American political beast.

Things Are Changing
06/30/2008

With the way the price of gas keeps rising, certain people are starting to change their minds on offshore drilling.

Over the last several terms of governorship in the state of Florida, the state leaders in the that state have been for the offshore ban that has existed since the Jimmy Carter administration.

The current governor, Charlie Christ, has come out for getting rid of that ban. By doing this, he has opened himself up to criticism from the environmentalist "wack-o's".

The facts are the facts. The higher prices keep going, the more people of every stripe will come over to the right side of the issue of drilling. This is an oil based economy.

Do The Believers Believe
07/01/2008

We see Barak Obama is attempting to reach out to many groups in order to appear to move to the political center. One of these groups is the conservative Christians.

The problem with this attempt is that his political beliefs are anything but conservative.

With religious friends like Reverend Jeremiah Wright, Michael Pfleger , and others preaching controversial sermons, I don't think he will be able to pull it off. James Dobson and other conservative Christian ministers are right in having serious questions on Obama.

Energy Moon Shot
07/02/2008

Our country has to be concerned with many different energy woes. What is definitely needed is and energy moon shot.

To correct our energy problem, we need to develope multiple forms of energy. We need to drill for more crude oil. That is more than a given. Without the oil, the current version of the automobile will not work. Oil is going to be the energy source for the engine of freedom for the foreseeable future; until other reliable sources are developed. We definitely need more nuclear power plants. If the French can do it, so can we. We have the room to put solar farms in the western part of our country. We need more hydroelectric dams. In terms of wind farms, people like the Kennedy's need to get over themselves and let the wind farms be built. Those wind farms could, at least, power the city of Hyannisport for years. Lastly, the development of renewable fuels needs to continued until they become more legitimate.

New oil resourses can be discovered much sooner than the people on the other side say that we can. Some of the so-called renewable fuels are at least ten or more years away. At this time, these renewable fuels are not economically feasible for the American general public to use. Until then, Americans will have to stick with oil.

We need as much oil as we can get, and as soon as we can get it.

Eyes On The Prize
07/03/2008

John McCain recently proposed to offer a $300 million prize to the person who would come up with the next great energy alternative.

That is all well and good, but what do we do until then? How long will this take and will it ever happen at all?

The fact that we still need to get the oil we need seems to elude McCain. It is generally believed it will take a very long time to get a total replacement for oil. Whereas, we need to keep using the kinds of energy sources we already have.

McCain needs to come fully over to the fact we need to drill because Barak Obama will not.

All Criticism Is Not The Same
07/04/2008

When the "Swift Boat Veterans for Truth" first appeared in 2004, they were speaking the truth. Criticism is not bad if it is the truth.

The problem is if one tries to criticize Barak Obama, even if it is true, they are told they are either racist or they are "swift boating" him. This is wrong. Criticism is one way political candidates can draw serious differences between themselves.

What would happen if some pastors that have worked with Obama when he was a community organizer, criticize him? Are they going to be discredited by saying they "swift boated" him?

The democrats will do anything to win the presidency.

One Step Closer
07/05/2008

It now seems the long-running cargo airport project that has been long-proposed to be built in Donaldsonville has jumped the last big hoop to become a project going from the drawing board to actually being built.

With the dissolving of the Louisiana Airport Authority into the newly formed Deportment of Economic Development, this means this airport is close to being built.

Along with Shintech and other proposals, this part of the state may be on the fast tract to growth. This several parish area has been one of the poorest parts of the state for a long time. It has been one of the areas that has been steadily losing population for a long time. Getting jobs to come here is a big deal.

We have seen several areas (Gonzales, Denham Springs) make overtures to big business. Why can't this area do the same?

What Iraqis Want
07/06/2008

It is nice to know that a Barak Obama presidency does not scares me. It scares the creeps out of the Iraqis on both sides of the ocean.

There is no doubt, in my mind, they are scared Obama will not want to finish the war and Iran might step into the power vacuum.

Everybody else in that world of the world hates the Americans. Iraq is a place that, as of now, the people like us. The other countries in that region are fearful of a free and democratic Iraq. If there is a successful, free and democratic Iraq, the people of the neighboring countries will see and want what Iraq will has.

The fact of the matter is that we are winning, and if we pull out too soon it will be like what happened after the first Gulf War. We lost a generation of Iraqis.

Both groups of Iraqis are right in praying for the election of John McCain.

Resignation
07/07/2008

Tommy Williams, Governor Bobby Jindel's legislative director, has recently resigned.

The job he has done for the governor is a mixed bag of results. He cannot be blamed for this because he is only doing what Jindal has directed him to do.

He did get the new ethics laws passed. The problem is that a majority of people think these laws have no teeth. As of this point in time they can't be enforced correctly because there are not enough people on the ethics board to do so. The case may be the people who have quit are the ones with ethics violations and they did not want those violations to come out.

This could be a good resignation. It might allow the governor to get a young person in place who will give him the ability to lobby and fight a legislature that might be against his reform agenda.

Tis' The Season
07/08/2008

Election season is fast approaching. This is the time of the year that will show us if Louisiana will remain a republican state or if it will become a democratic state.

Most people believe it will remain a republican one. For the most part, there aren't many races that have legitimate democrats running in them. The democrats running are the ones that are "conservative" ones or they have won recent special elections.

By far, the most important election is between Mary Landrieu and John Kennedy. We need Kennedy to win so we can get rid of the lady that is a part and parcel representation of machine politics in this state. She definitely represents the "Good Ole Boy" network.

The district that I live in is a conservative district. It suprised me to no end that Don Cazayoux won in this district. It was a good example of a democrat making who he really is an issue to get himself elected. It is, also, an example of the republicans getting behind a poor candidate. Woody Jenkins is a good person but a poor candidate. I hope Dr. Bill Cassidy can win this seat back because I don't trust Cazayoux to consistently vote conservatively. He is a democrat after all.

This will be an interesting election season.

Crime Bill
07/09/2008

Louisiana's Governor Bobby Jindal recently signed his crime bill into law. It seems to be a strong law, especially when in comes too child predators.

These people are monsters and need to be put away and chemically castrated. Those two things are in this bill. The problem comes when these people get released. No provisions has made for this. As long as they have their sick minds, they will do it again.

The other problem is what the Supreme Court has done to the Louisiana law that allows for the death penalty for child rapists. They muted it. They should not have done that. Of course, this comes from the liberal side of the Supreme Court. This can only be fixed by the election of John McCain to the office of the presidency.

Pitfalls Of Abortion
07/10/2008

There are a great deal of people who think that abortion is a bad thing. These pro-life people usually argue the issue from a moral and religious side. This is fine on the surface, but there are other sides to this issue. Lets focus on the political side.

This position is not whether or not to have the right to abortion. It is, also, not about when is or is not a fetus a life. What it is about is the fact that the more babies there are killed the more potential voters killed. This statistic may be an old one, but it is said that since abortion has become the a federal law in 1973, forty-five million babies have been aborted. Far be it for me to say that they all were from good loving couples. The facts state that some may well have been from evil people. On the other hand, I think that these are a minuscule amount. The vast majority might well have been from people that were good people that were forced to get an abortion because of "how it would look."

Let's say that 25% or 11,250,000 were from violent criminals and rapists. That leaves 33,750,000 babies that were aborted just because "it did not look good." These are babies that would have grown up and been on one side of the political debate or the other. These people would have, maybe, made it an easier win for George W. Bush or they may have put either Al Gore or John Kerry in the White House. In other words, abortion is killing voters.

It can't be argued that voters are important to the political process. We saw just how important it came to be in terms of the Louisiana legislatures idiotic idea for a 300% pay raise.

I will say it again, ABORTION KILLS VOTERS.

Bush Book
07/11/2008

If president George W. Bush were to write his memoirs after he leaves office, what might it include? That is a very good question.

One thing he might disclose is how to politically outmaneuver his political foes. It seems, at times, this was exactly what he did. This man is supposed to be a dolt. He is not supposed to be very smart, but he did out think his opponents on numerous issues.

He used kindness when it was warranted. This tactic disarmed them. He uses the bully pulpit of the presidency when all else failed. In some cases, he did what Ronald Reagan did and went over the congress's head, directly to the American people.

His memoirs should tell how he prosecuted the war on terror. It should ultimately tell the world it was right to go into Iraq. It will tell of the love and respect the Iraqis have for President George W. Bush.

It will tell of how he ran rings around the "mainstream" press. They really did not know what hit them. They are still punch drunk from their sparing sessions with this President. The press made every step of the way a struggle. They have second guessed his every move. They have shown their true colors.

After all is said and done, "My Presidency" by George W. Bush will stick it to the liberals in the biggest way of all. It will be a #1 best seller.

Gaming Veto
07/12/2008

Governor Bobby Jindal has vetoed a bill that would have allowed a horse racing track to have been built here in Iberville Parish. The problem is this track would have included slot machines, as well.

Jindel does not want to allow any more gaming to come into the state under his watch. This proposed track would have added more jobs to a state area that is, obviously, having a growth spurt.

At some point, this bill should be brought up again. Maybe, if it does not have the slot machines included in it, he won't veto it.

Niche Identification
07/13/2008

There are a number of black republicans saying they will vote for Barak Obama. This is something that I just don't get.

This is a man who believes in things that are diametrically opposed to conservatism. He is your typical post JFK democrat. He hates the military and wants to gut it. He wants to raise taxes to pre Ronald Reagan levels. Not spend is not an option for him. He is a BIG SPENDER.

This man would be extremely bad for the country.

Just because he is the first legitimate black candidate does not mean the African-Americans should vote for him. If they say they are conservatives, then they should not vote emotionally, racially, or impulsively.

Young Voters
07/14/2008

Will there be more young voters who will avail themselves of their responsibilities to vote? We will see.

Before an election, both sides believe a great number of the young people will vote. In most elections, this simply does not happen. This one could be different. As more and more "Rush" babies come of age, there is a great chance we may see them come out in droves.

The young of this nation have had their lives shaped by topics like Iraq, the war on terror, and high gas prices. There is just no telling how these people will vote. In general, the young vote democrat, but the "Rush" babies may have something to say about that.

The facts, the young probably won't affect the election very much. However, this election could prove to be different.

Qualifications
07/15/2008

On July fifth, the official election season began with the beginning of the qualification period.

This is the time when all politicians declare they are running for office. All offices from dog catcher to United States senator are included.

Some of the more cynical amongst us will say this is the period of time we see who will be "messing over us" for the next two to twelve years. I take the opposite stance. I think this is the time we see if we can replace the scoundrels with good people; and whether they can stay on the straight and narrow path. If the new people end up being scoundrels the process starts again.

That is the way this great country should work. I think like most elections, the number of voters will be extremely high. I also think more people care about political issues. It was evident by the way the people responded to the Louisiana legislative pay raise issue.

Those people who are up for reelection that supported the legislative pay raise, will be gone, and there is no doubt about it.

This will be a fun election to watch in the local, state, and federal areas.

Who's Who?
07/16/2008

In terms of immigration, John McCain is still for the "comprehensive" bill that has already failed. The proponents were not happy about this.

If McCain is elected president and continue to support this bill, he, along with a potential democratic congress will, again, try to bring that bill up again. There is a good shot if it is brought up again, the grass roots won't like it. This bill will probably pass because there won't be enough conservative votes against it in the legislature. This has created a scary situation. That is exactly why the voters need to put enough lawmakers in congress who agree with the grass roots; on both sides of the isle, to stop the bill.

Both Barak Obama and McCain are visiting Hispanic groups and promising to do this. This is one promise I hope McCain flip-flops on.

The Way It Should Be Done
07/19/2008

The Ouachita Economic Development Corporation is doing it the correct way. This is a civic minded group, that was put together to help develope the economics of a five parish area in the northeast part of Louisiana. They are raising money in a private way and not trying to ask the state government to foot the bill.

They could very easily be another one of these non-governmental organizations that would be considered pork, if they would ask for state tax money. Then ,what would probably happen, is at some point, the governor, whomever he might be, would have a tough decision to make. He might have to decide to cut off the funding to what could be a worthwhile organization.

I sincerely do wish those people well. They are trying to better themselves the correct way.

Corrections?
07/20/2008

What to do about the rising oil prices and the looming recession?

There is no easy answer to this question. Our problem stems from our reluctance to go after the natural resources that are rightfully ours.

Sure, the developing world is gobbling up energy at an increasing rate, but, why should that hurt us? It should not, but because of controllable factors we let spiral out of our hands, it has become an increasing annoyance. We could quickly relieve ourselves of the annoyance by doing whatever it takes to get our energy needs satisfied.

The first thing that needs to be done is to tell the environmentalist crazies to take a flying leap. There is no doubt in my mind they are hurting the country. Don't get me wrong, I want clean air and clean water, but at what cost. I think America is the best country to figure out a way to be able to have "their cake and eat it too". We have ways of getting to oil without dirtying up the environment. If God did not want us to use the oil, He would not have put it where we could find it; and made it in such an abundance supply

Another way for us to correct the problem is to "kick up" the other energy solutions. Such things like coal to oil and nuclear power need to be esculated. Again, the far-left environmentalists are in the way.

The next P.O.T.U.S. should make the same energy committment President John F. Kennedy made to the space program. This committment could have our country reducing, significantly, our oil needs in the next twenty years.

That is just some of the corrections needed to be made.

What Will Lieberman Do?.
07/21/2008

Senator Joe Lieberman has some big decisions to make.

We all know of the conflicts he has had with his party. Oh, they may say there is harmony, but I don't trust what the democrat are saying in response to this. If they did not dislike him, they would not have gone strongly after his seat in Connecticut. It certainly doesn't give him credibility with his party that he supports John McCain; and has been a hawk on the war on terror.

Even though I disagree with 95% of what he believes in, I have to give him the respect that he deserves. He believes what he believes and is not afraid to speak his mind.

I do not agree with him that he will not be considered by his party to be the vice president. What I do think is he will respectively decline, because it would more alienate him from his party.

Who Is John McCain?
07/22/2008

Who is John McCain's favorite president? He says his favorite is Theodore Roosevelt. We all know how Roosevelt ruled. He was not his cousin, FDR. He seemed to be more conservative. The man knew how to walk the line between accepting the money of the big business of his time and continue to keep those same big businesses (trust buster/manager.) He was an environmentalist that understood the oil business and knew how important "big oil" is to this country. Roosevelt understood national defense and knew that the country needs a strong military and military complex.

McCain thinks he fills most of that description to a tee. I am not so sure that I agree. On the environmental issues, I think this is one of the issues that separate him from "Teddy". Yes, Roosevelt created the boondoggle, that is the national parks system, the antiquities act, and the endanger species act. At the time he did this he did not foresee how people would be using those acts. He didn't see that these acts would be used to basically stop the oil companies from doing their jobs. McCain, at times, seems to want to keep the status quo. Then again, he flip-flops like a gymnast by ageeing with the American people by saying he would be willing to allow the drilling for crude oil. Other than that, he seems to walk the line with one of the greatest presidents in the history of America.

We are sorely in need of another Theodore Roosevelt.

What Must Be Done
07/23/2008

The Louisiana economy continues to be in poor shape. With all of the resources this state has, it could be the most economical state of the union.

The economic situation is being held back by greedy politicians. These politicians are so concerned about the pay raises for themselves they have forgotten about the harm they are doing to the state's economic growth. If the legislature would quit crying about their pay raises and do their jobs, maybe the economy would improve.

What needs to happen is to cut the business taxes. This would help to lure more businesses to this great state. Also, cut the state income tax. This would give more people the incentivive to go out and to get jobs.

It can't be argued things need to be done to correct a serious problem. Our lawmakers should set the example in good and wise money management.

The Made Man
07/24/2008

In the world of professional wrestling there was a performer with the moniker of "das wunderkind". This person was from Germany and his name was Alex Wright. What his name was supposed to mean was young, supremely talented performer and athlete.

Bobby Jindal, at least on the republican side of the isle, is the political version of this wrestler. This man has done so much in his young life that it is incredible. The man is, probably, headed to being president.

He needs to complete the job he has started. He promised the people of the state of Louisiana he would start the ball rolling on the long overdue great reform of the state. It is a reform that is long overdue and his national political aspirations can wait.

Even though there are some issues (legislative pay raises) the people of the state had to drag him by the nose to make the correct decision on, he eventually did make the right choice and remains in good graces with the people.

This man is definitely a high achiever and does not fit into the "lazy American" mold.

Within organized crime there is a term, "a made man." This means once a criminal gets into the hierarchy of a crime family, he is in there for life and can do his thing with impunity. Bobby Jindal is this person in terms of republican politics. There is no doubt in my mind, with him, the sky is the limit.

No, No, 1000 Times No
07/25/2008

Bobby Jindal has again said no to John McCain. McCain has repeatedly asked the governor to be the vice president in waiting. Over and over Bobby Jindal has said no. He has said this is the job that he wants an that he still has work to do as the governor of the state of Louisiana.

I definitely agree. This man has a great and tough job to do. Especially now that he has vetoed the legislative pay raises and the pork projects. The legislature has been crying over its lack of getting the pay raises and it now is throwing a tantrum over the governors cutting of those bills. These vetoed bill were ways lawmaker were buying votes with the government's money.

If Jindel took the offer from McCain he would look like a political opportunist. He has too much character and pride to do that to himself. He also knows this would cause him more problems with his electorate here in this state.

Why would he take the job when if he does a good job as the governor, he would get reelected? He would also, after two productive terms, be the same age as Barak Obama and would have a even greater shot of becoming president.

No Override
07/26/2008

Those legislators that are making a big stink about a veto override session are dumb and greedy. They are dumb because they do not understand the people siding with the governor to block this bill. Then, there is the greed factor. It is like "I want my money, I've got to have my money or I won't get reelected."

Some people say the governor did not do enough with his vetoes. He sent a message. The message is if these legislators send him bills with amendments in the them with requests for money in theme for such things as Joe Blow's charity for the blind or John Q's charity for the local church's social club, he will veto them.

That is the exact correct thing to do. If he does not continue to do this, the people will lose all respect for him. This proves Jindal is a man of character.

Cutting Off The Nose
07/27/2008

Sometimes the congress does things that are counterproductive. When it does these things, they usually end up hurting the country.

Case and point. Congress recently tried to pass a bill that would have forced oil companies to give up undrilled federal leases and ban the export of oil drilled in Alaska. The president threatened to veto it, which is exactly what he should have done if it had made it to his desk.

With the state of the economy at this time, we can't afford to not be drilling for and exporting oil out of Alaska.

What don't the democrats get? Energy is the biggest domestic issue that is out there.

They are, as they have done many times, cutting off their noses despite their faces. Is it no wonder the public's confidence level with the congress is at a historic low.

What The!
07/28/2008

What in the world are the democrats thinking? This could be a rhetorical question. Sometimes, I think these politicians aren't thinking and at times appear to be like a blonde, they appear to be air heads.

The democratic congress is rolling the dice. They are playing politics with the countries energy issue. They are hoping if the trends hold they will have a democratic president and a more democrat congress. They will open the country's drilling and tell their constituents in the environmental community to stuff it. By doing their business in this fashion, the democrats will get the credit for correcting this problem. That's what I call playing politics.

I still believe the GOP still has a shot to win at least part of the election, if not both. By focusing, directly, on the energy crisis they hope to not only reverse the trend, but also to gain enough seats in both houses of congress to get this issue settled. They hope to have the ability to block any potential policies put forth by Barak Obama. They need a veto-proof majority to get the job done.

The way the democrats work sometimes make me say WHAT THE!

More Dominoes Fall
07/29/2008

On July 21, the first domino fell in the Poverty Point Reservoir scandal. Lawyer Billy Coenen was arraigned at 10 am that day.

Along with Francis "The Fee" Thompson, Terry Denmon, and Thompson's brother Mike, they conspired to bilk the people of Louisiana out of a great deal of money. What those three men did was, is, and should have been a crime.

Mike Thomson and Denmon are to be arraigned on August 8th of this year.

What I am waiting for is what will eventually come; that is for one of these people to turn states evidence on "The Fee". That will be the most interesting thing for me. It will be fun for me to watch their little foursome disintegrate. When the feds get involve they don't stop until they get their man or men.

I think the governor should take state park hood away from Poverty Point and give that community the land. This would be a big way to call the legislature out. This would be be a big message to send.

Moscow and Havana
07/31/2008

Back in the 1960's Russia, known as the Soviet Union, tried to put missiles in Cuba. That resulted in the Cuban Missile Crisis. President John F. Kennedy stared them down and won.

As of this day, July 31, 2008, the Russians want to try to put a strategic bombing base in Cuba. We should not allow this to happen. This would definitely affect our national security.

The Russians don't like our plans to up missile defense stations in the former Soviet Union satellites. They also don't like the fact that we are getting close to Presiden Reagan's idea for a Strategic Defense Initiative (Star Wars).

If the Russians continue in this vain, there will be a big-time stand-off coming.

'Shale' We Do It
08/01/2008

Senator Mary Landrieu (D-La) is acting like a typical politician. She is saying one thing and doing another. She is saying that she wants to get as much oil as possible, but in the case of the oil shale, she voted with the less than distinguished gentleman from Colorado, Ken Salazar. Ken Salazar (D-Co) asked here to help bloc the ability block the ability to get the oil shale.

This is only one part of solving the current energy crisis. The problem is that the democrats are so beholden to the environmental lobby that nothing will get done.

Because of this, this is one of the most important national elections in recent history. All of the experts state this will be a democratic year, but the energy issue could change everything.

There could be a mistake by the republicans in bringing it up so late in the election cycle. That last statement could be wrong because you might not want to bring up an issue that might change a election too soon because the American people have a short term memory. With everything that is going on in their lives, people have only so much ram in their heads. You do not want them to forget the issue too soon. If they do, then the other side could obscure the facts and fool them. So I think the timing which the republicans brought it up at the exact correct time.

Let It Happen
08/02/2008

The idiots in congress are at it again. They want to pass a bill to clamp down on speculators. That is a needed legitimate job. Sure, there may be crooks in it but are there not crooks in the congress. Yes, commodities prices are artificially high. The markets will eventually correct themselves.

The speculations business is like being a bookie for commodities. They take money from people and bet that money on whether or not a specific commodity will go up or down. In general, a particular speculator does not, in and of him or herself, affect the market.

There is a reason the commodities market is called the futures market. The reason is that the bets are taken in order to predict what will happen in the future with a specific commodity.

Maliki's Vote
08/03/2008

Why Did the Prime Minister Do What He Did When Obama Visited Iraq?

There are several reasons for his actions. He may think his country is ready to be a sovereign, stand-alone country. Most do not agree with that assessment. There is a fifty-fifty chance the terrorists may regroup and come back stronger and we may have to go back in there. If we do, it could be even bloodier then it was the first time. He may also think his government is ready to go it alone. That, too, may be the case, but we will see. Until it is deemed the governmental officials can do their jobs without fear of being killed by insurgents, then he should keep his mouth shut.

Maliki likes Obama's 16-month plan because it gets America out as soon as possible.

I don't like it for several reasons. First and foremost, Obama is not asking for any military bases there. That is not a good idea because Iraq is in a strategic place for us to keep an eye on Iran. Secondly, we need to have a staging area for any operations that need to be carried out in the middle east. About Obama, I will say it again, he is of the current crop of democrats. They hate and loathe anything that has to do with the military and will cut their funding when the chance comes.

I like that Maliki is generally on America's side. I am glad he has no vote in the election. I know one thing for sure, the Iraqi's living here in America, don't think they can bring themselves to vote for Obama. The reason is they have heard the democrats spew all of their bile about the war.

Scare Tactic
08/04/2008

The democrats are at it again. Then want the fairness doctrine reinstated and they are one election away from getting it done.

They want to protect themselves and their buddies in the mainstream. They want it to go back to what it was before Rush Limbaugh came onto the scene. The democrats want to give out their stories and run with them. Because there was no one to refute the so-called facts, they could get away with lies. The democrats could release information about their bad bills and the press would ultimately spin it into something good, at least for the democrats.

Things actually started to change when, a few years before Rush, the fairness doctrine was smacked down by the courts. Now, there is not only talk radio, but, also the internet, and Fox News. There is also a growing amount of conservative newspapers that have, lately, come onto the scene.

It is so obvious what the liberals want to do. They want to shut the conservatives up. They want their media monopoly back and they are bound and determined to get it back.

This election is important for a multitude of reasons, the least of which is the un-fairness doctrine.

Obama, A Bad Bet
08/05/2008

Some of the big money people on the democratic side of the isle think Barak Obama is a bad bet. What that means is he is not getting their money. That does not matter. He is amassing most of his money from the internet.

The reason he has not been getting money from the big money people is that they get the feeling he is not going to sustain his trajectory. They think he has piqued too early.

I can't say that I disagree.

The more things that get revealed, the more votes he seems to lose. He doesn't have to worry about the African-American vote. He also has the young vote. The problem comes with the blue collar vote. He also is losing the vote of the older women.

Those are the problems he is having. If he can't correct these problems, he is going to lose the election, and in a big way.

In The Past
08/06/2008

Barak Oabam was in Hawaii on Tuesday, July 27, 2008, to speak to some minority reporters. He was there to apologize for the way our country has treated the American Indians. Sure, we have treated them poorly, especially making them walk on the Trail of Tears, where thousands of them died. That was wrong.

There, also, were wrongs committed by the original native Americas. Chiefs amongst them orchestrated big and crooked land deal. Without proof of ownership, they sold the land that eventually became the state of New York.

All I am saying is that crimes were done on both sides. Apologies need to be forthcoming from both sides.

For Or Against
08/07/2008

We know where both sides of the isle stand on the Fairness Doctrine. The democrats are for it because they want their buddies in the mainstream media to have their monopoly and they want to control all the information about the issues. Even though they have been hammered on specific issues by the people on talk radio and the blogs, the republicans are against it.

Barak Obama has said that he is against it, but, if he were to win and the democrats were to take congress with bigger margins, you can book it he would sign the Fairness Doctrine back into law.

This is a definite assault on the constitution.

Shut Down Coming
08/08/2008

There is a definite shot that the oil issue will cause a shut down of the federal government. I am not so sure this would not be a good thing. If it is shut down, then it is not doing things to hurt us. Sure, people like government employees, welfare recipients, and social security recipients will not receive their checks. In the case of the governmental workers it is unfair because these people are just doing their jobs, even though some of them may need to be cut.

This oil thing is not going away. It will be a huge issue in the election, especially with the fact the north, when the election happens, will be in the throws of another bitter winter. Heating oil has gone up and I think some people will find they will have to make some tough choices.

It is the correct thing to do for the republicans. For them to have a shot at taking the congress, they needed one issue that a majority of the American agree upon.

I definitely think a federal shut down is a better than even bet (about 65%) to happen.

Race Based
08/09/2008

A major base of Barak Obama's presidential campaign is centered around race. The more the people supporting him say it is not, the more the opposite looks like it is true.

The man wants to be the first black president. All of his supporters are making a big deal of saying that if he does not get elected, it will set race relations back in our great country. I think this is not a good platform to run on. The facts has proven that the further away from the 1960's we get, the less racist the country gets. Sure, there will always be a select group of people that hate, but that group has gotten to where is has very little power.

As the American generations roll one, the less race seems to matter. There are racists on both sides. The white racist, we know where they stand. We know where the black racists stand as well. Both are causing a great amount of harm.

In Trouble
08/10/2008

Could Mary Landrieu be in trouble?

The answer to that is absolutely.

This election is a very important one. We, as a country, can't afford for Barak Obama to win and for the democrats to make their margins bigger in both of the house of congress. This election could ruin this country in more ways than one could imagine.

Back to Landrieu. As much as she wants to convince people otherwise, she IS one of the most liberal senators in the United States Senate. All one has to do is to look at her voting record and that point gets driven home hard. Also, look at another senator she has sided with in the senate, Senator Salazar (D-Co). He asked her to oppose drilling for the oil shale in his home state of Colorado. The sad part is she agreed. She favors high taxes. She wants nationalized medicine. The nationalized medicine thing would be a killer because the quality of services would go down. We would end up looking a lot like Great Britain and Canada.

These are some of the reason Landrieu should be defeated in the up and coming eledtion. She has not be good for Louisiana and for our country. Our future as a country is in a perilous position.

Vietnam Vets Help Defend Freedom, Again
08/11/2008

We owe the veterans of Vietnam a great debt. These men and women are helping to defend freedom once again. They, in their youth, went off the fight and did not get the respect due to them when they returned. That was a sad part in the history of our great nation. That was the only war our fighting forces did not get the heroes welcome upon their return. Because of the peace-nick, dome smoking FM type, good time rock and rollers, these soldiers were not treated the way other returning warriors were treated.

These men and women are not going to let this happen to the current group of returning servicemen. They think, and rightly so, the soldiers, seamen, fly boys, and marines should not be treated in the deplorable fashion as they were treaed. I can't say that I disagree with them. That is why I agree with everything they are doing. They protect the funerals of the fallen heroes. They also organize counter protests to go against the ones staged by groups, such as Code Pink.

By doing what they are doing, they insure that we never lose respect for what the armed forces are doing to secure the safety of the greatest country on the face of the earth.

Where's The Help
08/12/2008

There was supposed to be a coalition of the willing when we went into Iraq. The country of Georgia was one of the participants. I agree with their people when they said, "we helped in Iraq, where is the West."

The great bear is on the march and it seems it will not stop until it has all of the power in the region. The cold war looks like it is kicking up again, but the Russians are looking for economic power as well as military power. They want the control of all of the oil in the region, except the oil of their friends, the Iranians and Chinese.

We need to, somehow, find a way to help the Georgians. They are, definitely, a fighter of terror and they want to stay free.

Divided?
08/13/2008

Are the republicans as divided as Sarah Chacko alleges in her article "Democrats, GOP sharply divided." Sure, there are republicans that are trying to sabotage their own party. I think the majority of GOP want to drill for crude oil as much as possible.

While there are forty or so house republicans making their point with protest, there are also five senators in the so-called "Gang of Ten" capitulating they might have undercut their "friends" in the house. I don't get why Lindsay Graham and the other four republicans on the "Gang of Ten" are some of the ones killing the party by bending over and letting the democrats perform a rectal exam.

Those five republicans do not seem to care about the polls, stating the American people do not want a limited drilling bill. They want to get as much oil from as may places as possible. The democrats do not seem to get that either.

This is the reason Mary Landrieu, Don Cazayoux, and the rest of the democrats are running for the United States Congress in the great state of Louisiana. Landrieu has made some peculiar decision that fly in the face of her claiming she is for drilling. She voted for NOT going after the oil shale. Cazayoux has made a very bad decision when he voted to cut off debate and to shut down the house for their August vacation.

When Cazayoux got elected he said he was not going to be a puppet for Nancy Pelosi. That was a lie. I think, much like the rest of democrats in Louisiana, both of these candidates will get beat bad.

Message Sent, Message Received
08/14/2008

When the Russians went into the country of Georgia there was a message in it. The message is, "the Russian Bear is back". It is evident they have been back for a long time. They have been flying their strategic bombers and the KGB have been killing their political enemies as in the days of the communists.

It can not be argued the country of Georgia is a friend of America and friend of freedom. America must protect her friends.

The Russians are wanting to bow themselves up an prove they are back as a superpower. The do have a strong military, but that is not where it is the strongest. They have a very strong economy due to their oil supply. That is what is scary about it.

They have designs of bringing all of the former Soviet satellites back.

The problem is the countries in that area of the world have tasted freedom and do not want to give it up. We need to do whatever is possible to keep those people free. We need to invoke aggressive containments. These containments should not be carried out by diplomacy alone. There needs to be, not only, humanitarian aid, but also military aid. It may come to bite us in the future (see Bin-Laden), but this may, very well, be a different case.

I definitely think the message was sent and was well received.

Southern Hollywood
08/15/2008

There is definitely a creative bias in Hollywood. Conservatives can not come out politically unless they have won awards or are well established.

Big changes are soon to occur. There is an incredible growth in the movie industry in Louisiana. There could be an onrush of conservatives in the movie industry who may want to continue to work. Relocating to Louisiana may be a good decision for these people. I understand actors and actresses want to be loved by their peers, they are human after all.

It is about time to see conservative actor not to be couched in super hero movies and fantasy movies. It is also time for actors like Kelsey Grammar, Patricia Heaton, Tom Selleck, and others get the big movie rolls. What about writers like Ben Stein? This man is brilliant person. If he writes a script, he needs to have it looked at as seriously as one written by Penny Marshal.

The Louisiana movie industry could change things, big time. They are as far away from Hollywood as you possibly can be, and they can hire Louisiana people to do all things from running the studio to the studio guards. These people, even though they may be democrats, they are the more conservative ones.

On The Horizon
08/16/2008

The election is the eight-hundred pound gorilla in the room. Even though there has been a slight drop is the price per barrel of oil, decreases in price will not go into effect until sometime down the line. The prices will remain high and the pressure the republicans are applying will not go away.

The folks are mad and will remain that way. The more the democrats are stubborn on this issue, the more angry the American people are getting.

The democrats are full of themselves and a little bit too over confident. The pundits on their side of the isle are still predicting an incredible victory. What usually happens when an athlete gets too confident and lets his mouth overload his behind? In the case of the singular sports the athlete loses; and, in the case of the team sports, the athlete's team loses.

The democrats better watch themselves. If they are not careful, their perfectly laid plans will be ruined by the American people. The American people are, very much, frustrated. They tried to give the republicans a shot at correcting the problems. It did not work. Now the democrats are failing, in spectacular fashion as well.

If, somehow, the republicans can pull off what would be considered a spectacular upset, they can't get full of themselves either. If they do, they will end up the same as the democrats. If the cycles keep repeating, there will come a time when there will be a viable third party; and it will get its chance to do something positive.

What's on the horizon in terms of oil? As I see it, there will be a slight easing in price, but it will remain high. There is also a shot the people will switch back to their habits before the high prices hit.

Again, we need to increase supply. We have yet to do so. Sure, the price has come down, but what will happen during the winter when there is more usage? I fear the slight lessening in prices will be negated. If that is the case, all of the "hard work" of the democrats will be up in smoke, and it will eventually cost them their power. It will also hurt them down the line and they may have to restructure their party. It may also cost them the ability to have a president elected from their side of the isle for a couple of generations.

Orthodox Church's Plea
08/17/2008

The Orthodox Christian Church of Russian has made a plea. It would like to see all hostilities stopped and everything figured out peacefully.

What else can the leader of that church say? No Christian wants to see anybody of the same faith or of any other faith killed.

The facts are that as long as Vladimir Putin is the defacto Czar, that particular set of circumstances will not present itself.

Putin is your, basic, all-powerful dictator who wants to control everything, and that includes religion.

After everything is said and done with these former Soviet Satellites, the Russian Ortodox Church better watch itself.

What's Up In The North
08/18/2008

The United States is sending a geological mapping service to map the Arctic Continental Shelf. The reason is to find the potentiality of oil reserves there. The Russians have already "claimed" 420,000 miles of the ocean floor, and we just can't allow them to find all the oil there; that is, if there is any.

The Russians are already oil rich and that is why they can flex their military and economic muscles. The more they do that (flex their muscles), the more they will become a major threat, not only in the area, but also in the world

The American people, when polled, by the amount of 70% to 30%, want to get as much oil as this country can find. They don't want to have to deal with high fuel prices, ever again.

End Game Is Coming
08/19/2008

I have said it before, "Americans like to win." What this means is that in any part of life the American citizenry likes to win.

The Iraq war is no different. We seem to be on the way to winning it. Sure, the government's part of the solution is slowing things down, but that is the case with big government. In a few years, there may be a time when the Iraqi people become disenchanted with their government. They will have the ability to change it.

They actually love America and the majority of its ideals. It would hurt the good people of Iraq if we pulled out too early. We would, much like in the first Gulf War, lose a great deal of the support of the citizenry of Iraq. That would kill our goals.

Barak Obama and the democrats still seem to want to leave before the job is done. This war could be academic after the election and they may eventually get their way. They just need to be patient and let the job get done. The democratic president and the democratic controlled congress should not cut the military budget; because if they do, there could be some attacks that have heretofore not occurred.

Our young men and women in the military have done their jobs magnificently. We should be very proud of them, and for the most part, we are. We are currently turning around the military's mistakes of the last two democratic presidents. The majority of our current problems stem from the foreign policy mistakes made by Jimmy Carter. Case and point is the Shaw of Iran. He may not have been the perfect leader, but he was a westward looking Iranian. When Carter made the mistake of supporting the Mullahs, he sent this country on the course ending with American attacking Iran.

I really do think that the end game is near.

Lot More To Cut
08/20/2008

A few weeks back, Governor Bobby Jindal cut $40+ million dollars of funding for parks. But there is a nasty little secret, there are millions more to cut. Here is, according to CB Forgoston, a comprehensive list:

EFFORTS OF GRACE, INC.
Ashe Too, Planning and Construction (Orleans)
Payable from General Obligation Bonds
Priority 1 $910,000

LIGHTHOUSE FOR BLIND IN NEW ORLEANS
Economic Development Project, Planning and Construction (Jefferson, Lafourche, Orleans, Plaquemines, St. Bernard, St. Charles, St. James, St. Tammany, Terrebonne, Washington)
Payable from General Obligation Bonds
Priority 1 $1,100,000

RENAISSANCE HOME FOR YOUTH
Renaissance Education Building, Planning and Construction (Rapides)
Payable from General Obligation Bonds
Priority 1 $1,320,000

YMCA OF THE CAPITAL AREA
North Baton Rouge YMCA, Planning and Construction (East Baton Rouge)
Payable from General Obligation Bonds
Priority 1 $350,000

DISTRICT 2 ENHANCEMENT CORPORATION
St. Claude Community Development and Beautification Project, Planning and Construction (Orleans)
Payable from General Obligation Bonds
Priority 1 $300,000

COMMUNITY DEVELOPMENT AND BEAUTIFICATION PROJECT, PLANNING, ACQUISITION AND CONSTRUCTION (ORLEANS)
Payable from General Obligation Bonds
Priority 1 $250,000

NEW ORLEANS EAST WALKING AND BIKE TRAIL, PLANNING AND CONSTRUCTION (ORLEANS)
Payable from General Obligation Bonds
Priority 1 $400,000

TECHE ACTION BOARD, INC.
Franklin Expansion St. Mary Parish Location for the Purchase and Renovation of an Existing Building and to Renovate the Current Facility, Planning and Construction (St. Mary)
Payable from General Obligation Bonds
Priority 1 $1,450,000

ARC OF NORTH WEBSTER
New Roof Construction and Existing Building Modifications, Planning and Construction (Webster)
Payable from General Obligation Bonds
Priority 1 $150,000

RECONCILE NEW ORLEANS, INC.
Reconcile New Orleans, Renovation and Expansion Project, Central City New Orleans, Planning and Construction (Orleans)
Payable from General Obligation Bonds
Priority 1 $625,000

LITTLE THEATRE OF SHREVEPORT
Little Theatre of Shreveport, Planning and Construction (Caddo)
Payable from General Obligation Bonds
Priority 1 $1,300,000

GREATER URBAN LEAGUE OF NEW ORLEANS
The Urban League of Greater New Orleans Building Renovations (Orleans)
Payable from General Obligation Bonds
Priority 1 $200,000

TANGIPAHOA AFRICAN-AMERICAN HERITAGE MUSEUM AND BLACK VETERANS ARCHIVES
Tangipahoa African-American Heritage Museum and Black Veterans Archives (Tangipahoa)
Payable from General Obligation Bonds
Priority 1 $50,000

BATON ROUGE CASA
Baton Rouge CASA Facility, Acquisition, Design, Planning and Construction (East Baton Rouge)
Payable from General Obligation Bonds
Priority 1 $250,000

7TH DISTRICT BAPTIST ASSOCIATION
Roof Replacement and Repairs and Equipment to Christian Villa Nursing Home, Planning and Construction (Acadia)
Payable from General Obligation Bonds
Priority 1 $260,000

OPTIONS, INC.
Safe Haven Multi-Purpose Vocational Center and Shelter, Planning and Construction (Tangipahoa)
Payable from General Obligation Bonds
Priority 1 $500,000

LOUISIANA MILITARY HALL OF FAME & MUSEUM, INC.
Museum (Vermilion)
Payable from General Obligation Bonds
Priority 1 $100,000

EAST CARROLL COUNCIL ON AGING
East Carroll Voluntary Council on Aging Renovation, Planning and Construction (East Carroll)
Payable from General Obligation Bonds
Priority 1 $50,000

MAGNAVILLE LOUISIANA, USA, INC.
Multipurpose Evacuation Shelter/Community Center in Simmesport, Acquisitions, Utilities, Planning and Construction (Avoyelles)
Payable from General Obligation Bonds
Priority 1 $400,000

LOUISIANA ALLIANCE OF BOYS & GIRLS CLUBS
Louisiana Alliance of Boys and Girls Club, Inc., Planning, Acquisitions, and Construction (Statewide)
Payable from General Obligation Bonds
Priority 1 $100,000

BOGALUSA YMCA
Bogalusa YMCA, Master Planning, Design, Construction, Renovations and Equipment Acquisitions (Washington)
Payable from General Obligation Bonds

Priority 1 $75,000

ST. MARY COMMUNITY ACTION AGENCY
Office Addition and Modifications for Community Action Agency, Planning and Construction (St. Mary)
Payable from General Obligation Bonds
Priority 1 $560,000

ST. TAMMANY PARISH EVENTS DISTRICT
East St. Tammany Events Center, Planning, Designing and Construction (St. Tammany)
Payable from General Obligation Bonds
Priority 1 $5,000

LOUISIANA BLACK HISTORY HALL OF FAME
Museum and Cultural Center, Planning and Construction (East Baton Rouge)
Payable from General Obligation Bonds
Priority 1 $350,000

TREME COMMUNITY EDUCATION PROGRAM
Leverette Senior House, Planning and Construction (Orleans)
Payable from General Obligation Bonds
Priority 1 $420,000

Program Operations, Planning, Acquisitions, Renovations and/or Construction (Orleans)
Payable from General Obligation Bonds
Priority 1 $ 50,000

FAMILY CENTER OF LIFE, INC.
Family Center of Hope Community Center in New Orleans, Planning and Construction (Orleans)
Payable from General Obligation Bonds
Priority 1 $100,000

ARC OF GREATER NEW ORLEANS
Restoration of the Fontana Center of the ARC of Greater New Orleans in Metairie, Planning and Construction (Jefferson)
Payable from General Obligation Bonds
Priority 1 $150,000

HOME AWAY FROM HOME, INC.
Purchase and Installation of Emergency Generators (Washington)
Payable from General Obligation Bonds
Priority 1 $90,000

WASHINGTON PARISH FAIR ASSOCIATION
Renovations to Historic Buildings, Planning and Construction (Washington)
Payable from General Obligation Bonds
Priority 1 $50,000

ARC OF OUACHITA
Emergency Shelter and Therapeutic Center for the Developmentally Disabled, Acquisition, Planning, Construction and Renovation (Ouachita)
Payable from General Obligation Bonds
Priority 1 $100,000

NEW ORLEANS NEIGHBORHOOD DEVELOPMENT
NDF Homeownership Center, Planning and Construction (Orleans)
Payable from General Obligation Bonds
Priority 1 $350,000

TRINITY CHRISTIAN COMMUNITY
Carrollton Community Center Renovations, Land Acquisition, Site Work, Planning and Construction (Orleans)
Payable from General Obligation Bonds
Priority 1 $1,075,000

NEW ORLEANS MUSIC HALL OF FAME
South Rampart Street Historic Development Project, Planning and Construction, (Orleans)
Payable from General Obligation Bonds
Priority 1 $2,000,000

ASSUMPTION PARISH COUNCIL ON THE AGING, INC.
Council on Aging Building, Planning and Construction (Assumption)
Payable from General Obligation Bonds
Priority 1 $960,000

TRIUMPH OF SPECIAL PEOPLE, INC.
Housing for Disabled Recipients of Waiver Services, Acquisition, Planning and Construction (Jefferson)
Payable from General Obligation Bonds
Priority 1 $370,000

LOUISIANA 4-H FOUNDATION
Louisiana 4-H Foundation Youth Educational Development Center, Camp Windy Wood Property (Grant)
Payable from General Obligation Bonds
Priority 1 $250,000

YMCA OF GREATER NEW ORLEANS

New Westbank YMCA (Jefferson)
Payable from General Obligation Bonds
Priority 1 $700,000

DRYADES YMCA
Technical Training Center, Planning and Construction (Orleans)
Payable from General Obligation Bonds
Priority 1 $1,000,000

DRYADES YMCA RECONSTRUCTION, PLANNING AND CONSTRUCTION,
PLANNING AND RECONSTRUCTION (ORLEANS)
Payable from General Obligation Bonds
Priority 1 $1,500,000

COMMUNITY OUTREACH PROGRAMS
Willow Glen River Road Senior Resource Center, Planning, Construction and Equipment
(Rapides)
Payable from General Obligation Bonds
Priority 1 $1,270,000

LOUISIANA LEADERSHIP INSTITUTE
Multi-Purpose Education Enrichment Center Athletic Field, and Band Room, Planning and
Construction (East Baton Rouge)
Payable from General Obligation Bonds
Priority 1 $1,000,000

NORTHEAST DELTA RC&D
Franklin Parish Activity Center, Planning and Construction (Franklin)
Payable from General Obligation Bonds
Priority 1 $325,000

ALLUME SOCIETY
Frank's Theatre Restoration, Planning, Acquisition, Renovation, and Construction (Vermilion)
Payable from General Obligation Bonds
Priority 1 $100,000

SCHEPIS FOUNDATION, INC.
Schepis Building Renovations, Planning and Construction (Caldwell)
Payable from General Obligation Bonds
Priority 1 $450,000

LONGUE VUE HOUSE AND GARDENS
Restoration and Master Site Planning (Orleans)
Payable from General Obligation Bonds
Priority 1 $100,000

MERCY ENDEAVORS
Irish Channel St. Andrew Street Elderly Resource Center (Orleans)
Payable from General Obligation Bonds
Priority 1 $205,000

RED RIVER REVEL ARTS FESTIVAL
Covered Pavilion #2 for Shreveport Festival Plaza, Planning and Construction (Caddo)
Payable from General Obligation Bonds
Priority 1 $250,000

MULTICULTURAL TOURISM COMMISSION
C.C. Antoine Museum and Arts Center, Planning and Construction (Caddo)
Payable from General Obligation Bonds
Priority 1 $305,000

The Grand Total for these NGO's/pork is $18,345,000 .00. That is still way to much. You have to understand that the next Capital Outlay bill will have these pork projects in it plus some that are new. Will the Governor Bobby Jindel have a pair of grapefruits big enough to cut these, plus the new ones that are sure to appear? We will see.

Bait And Switch
08/21/2008

Politicians are almost as bad as lawyers. We all know just how many jokes are out there about attorneys being less that ethical and lower than slime.

The big lie has been told about the Stelly Tax. The lie is the tax payers will get it January 1, 2009. That is not the case. They have set it up to where the people will not get it until 2010.

After all the work the people did to get the cut as soon as possible, to have them change the timing is a slimy move. But, that is to be expected from the current political creatures. They set it up this way so that, in an election year, they can say they have given the people a tax cut.

I am not so sure the change that should be made, will be made. I think the lawmakers want it the was it is. I think the people will have to get in gear like they did with the legislative pay raise issue.

Fun Time
08/22/2008

For me, the drama the democrats are waging in the primaries is very enjoyable. This drama is sure to spill over at the democratic convention. The fact of the matter is that even though Barak Obama has capitulated to the Clintons and appears to have been made to look weak, he is still the presumptive democratic nominee.

The odds of the planned protests getting out of hand are very high. There are a lot of unhappy democrats that are not very happy about Hillary Clinton not being the presumptive nominee.

The last time this same situation presented itself was in 1968. It was an ugly situation made even uglier because of the television cameras. Sure, it made for great television, but the party's big wigs did not want that to happen. They wanted a boring, sterile convention.

Sometimes, when you want something bad, the opposite happens. Even though there has been a lot of giveaways by Barak Obama, there will be hundreds of thousands of people outside and inside of the arena that are not going to be happy with the pick of the party. They want their person in.

I will be very happy and filled with enjoyment if and when the coming to pass of degenerating democratic convention shows itself on televison. There is a great chance there could be tasers, tear gas, and arrests. And, it will be fun to watch.

Riding Saddleback
08/23/2008

Recently, both presidential candidates appeared at Rick Warren's Saddleback Church forum.

Barak Obama did not do very well. He seem to have very detailed answers that appeared to go over the heads of the average American. The answers he gave also seemed convoluted. It should not surprise people that this was the case, because he is vacuous and vapid. This candidate can not survive without a teleprompter.

John McCain, on the other hand, came off looking like a very deep and serious person. His answers were concise, to the point and understandable to the "regular" people. This is a very deed person whose experiences have shaped his life and would shape the presidency. He was quick to answer the questions, even though some people could have disliked the answers, everyone now knows where he stands.

McCain rode the horse at Saddleback like he was a real cowboy and Obama rode like the city person he is.

Mistake
08/24/20008

This is a red statement that is getting redder by the moment. It is amazing a liberal politician could actually win an election by lying about who he is and what he believes.

Case and point, Mary Landerieu. She says she is for certain programs but her voting record show just the opposite.

She is running like the dickens away from her party's nominee for P.O.T.U.S. It is generally considered he will not do very well in November. I can understand why she would want to run from him. Sure, she may agree with and, in a vast majority of cases, vote for his initiatives, but because of where she is from, she has to appear she is "conservative."

I don't think this strategy will work. It might have worked before Rita and Katrina, but not post storm. Again, she has a long unfavorible voting record and voters should seriously examine it.

National Debt
08/25/2008

Debt is debt. Our country is having the same debt problems that some individual Americans are having. It is good idea that John McCain has added deficit hawk Richard Viguerie to his staff.

This national deficit is killing the country. It could be even worse if the democrats take the entire ball of wax. That is a very scary thought.

We know what Barak Obama wants to do. He wants to raise taxes to help pay for his risky schemes. Raising taxes is always a bad idea. This hurts everyone.

But I digress.

I don't think you can get rid of the deficit in one fell swoop. It's going to take time. There is so much waste in the government that it isn't funny. If McCain gets control of the waste, then that will go a long way to lowering the deficit. Sure, we have a trade deficit. But, it can be remedied by us making better quality products. That is better said than done.

The Shield Is Coming
08/26/2000

The United States recently put up the two parts of a proposed eastern European missile shield. This is not making the Russians too happy. Screw the Russians.

If you really look at it, the Russians brought this on themselves. They are attacking sovereign countries, and threatening others (the eastern block nations). These former satellites want to remain free.

We, as a nation, have a responsibility to protect burgeoning democracies everywhere. If we do not, we are not doing our job. The Russians are thinking, and rightfully so, that they are a superpower. They are awash in oil money and also in arms money. They sell products to Iran, China, and others countries considered enemies of freedom.

This is the opening salvo in another cold war. It does not bode well for Israel. There are alliances coming together for the biblical battle of Armageddon.

Union Greed
08/27/2008

The work unions are acting like the fascists that they are. They want to take away the private vote from their members. We all know they are in the tank for the democrats; and if the democrats take the White House and get a bigger majority in the congress, the national union leaders will be able to bully and intimidate their rank into voting the way the leaders want their members to vote.

I think that, for the most part, the members of unions think the same way on most of the issues. The rank and file should have the right to vote in private, for or against, any issue or candidate. These are good people and their rights should not be trampled on. I sincerely hope some person that is in the rank and file sues. If this law goes through this could be a serious constitutional issue.

I think that if the unions are allowed to take away the votes of their members, what come next?

Conservation, Yeah Right
08/28/2008

The crude oil price continues to go up and down. This will continue as long as the United States government is not getting serious about going and getting our own oil reserves.

The arguments continue on whether or not to drill. The problem is the more time the democratic idiots continue to argue, the more the people are hurt. When the people are hurt and angry, they may approach their politician, as they did in days gone by, with torches and pitchforks.

The thing that scares me is the fortunes of our energy policy could go different ways. If the democrats take everything, the amount of stockpiles will not change, but the amount used, because of the seasonal change, will change. Winter will hold the key.

Usually, the voters are satisfied with the congressmen and representatives they voted for and not with the others' lawmakers. Now, it seems the people are unhappy with all lawmakers.

This is a real problem for the democrats because they are the ones that are standing in the way of getting the oil the country needs and it could cost them in a big, big way.

Acceptance
08/29/2008

Barak Obama made his acceptance speech last night. He finally made some specific promises. These promises scare me.

His plans for our wallets scare me. He wants to "raise taxes on the rich." Does he not under stand if he does raise taxes, he will adversely hurt the economy? The democrats are always targeting the "richest 1%". Does he not understand the money which is not spent in paying taxes is reinvested back into the business? It may go for update of equipment, expansion, or more personnel. High taxes has a counter effect. Increases means many businesses will be forced to lay off workers. If the government wants more revenues coming into the federal system, taxes need to be kept low. More people paying less taxes will bring in more money than less people paying more taxes.

Obama would like to see high taxes so he can have the money to spend on liberal programs.

What really scares me is that he wants to throw some more money at education. More money does not mean better quality in educaton. Paying teachers more does not fix education in the inner city schools because no matter what teachers are paid, good teachers cannot be kept. Obama wants to end the talk of vouchers, so as not to allow students the choice of private, parochial, home schools, and home school co-operatives. They want those students in troubled public school to continue to fail. Pouring tax money into these public school pacifies the parents of the children, and they believe they are getting something. In essence, the democrats are doing this because they want to continue to get the votes. The children are the ones suffering for this "hard headed" way of thinking.

Those are just two of the issues that Obama talked about in his acceptance speech.

The World's Bullies
08/30/2008

There are bullies everywhere in the world. If we are to listen to the democratic nominee for vice president, Joe Biden, about foreign policy, we will need to bloody some noses.

As of this point-in-time, there is one major bully on the block that may end up posing a threat to the United States. It is Vladimir Putin. This leader is bulling the former Russian satellite nations to try to get them go come back under Russian control. This threatens democracy everywhere, and especially in Europe. He needs to be taught a lesson. His nose needs to be bloodied. Out country should issue some extreme economic sanctions against Russia, to the point his people would want to remove him from his office. This will let him know we mean business. It is meant to say we can still, if you will beg my pardon, reach out and touch him.

China is trickier. We trade a great deal with them and a bunch of our countries have manufacturing factories there. Something needs to be done about their human rights abuses. Do we have the guts to do it? I don't know.

Hugo Chavez is going down the road which will lead to his destruction. He is trying to bring back communism. This will never work. He wants total control of all media in Venezuela. The people are trying to keep him in check, but may not be able to do it without outside help.

All of these two-bit dictators will get theirs soon. Just how soon will that be? I don't know.

They all, definitely, need their noses bloodied.

Justice Will Come
08/31/2008

We all know New Orleans is the cesspool of politics. It has been ruled for forty or more years by the democrat. Republicans may not have done any better, but certianly, it is now time to rid it from the corruption.

Case in point is, William "Cold Cash" Jefferson. This is a man who was caught hiding $100,000 of illegal money in his freezer. Of course, he denied it, but he was caught red handed. He is not the only one in his family that is in serious trouble. His older brother, Moses, is facing corruption charges. His sister and her daughter were also charged with corruption. Their parents must be proud.

Back to "Cold Cash." This man just got reelected and, for the life of me, I don't know why. There could be several things at work here. He could be one of these politicians that says, "Look at what I helped to bring home". Also, he could, like some other democrats, have paid people to vote for him. Surely, this would be voter fraud. Finally, it could be a combination of all of these factors. Whatever it is, the longer he is in office, the more he damages the reputation of the city and the state.

My sincere hope is that one of his opponents, in the democratic primary, or the general election, beats him soundly. Certainly, we trust an honest judge will be on the bench when he goes to trial in federal court.

He, and all of his corrupt family members need to go to jail, and for a long time.

Ethics Nominations
09/01/2008

Even though there are some who say the new ethics laws are still too laxed, defending them is difficult because there aren't enough persons to defend them.

The fact of the matter is that the people that quit the ethics board are like a children on the playground who do not want to share. If thing do not go his way, he will take his toy and go home.

We all should say, "Good riddance to these people. If they don't want to help take the state in a new direction, then, we should be happy to see them gone. It now appears the ones who quit were part of the problem. They seemed to be part of the the "Good Ole Boy" network.

These removals should root out the rottenness. We trust that those replacing them will have high standards and ideals.

In Memoriam
09/11/2008

This is the three year anniversary of the worst attack on American soil since Pearl Harbor. We will always remember 9/11. This brings home the fact that there are two different ways, with two different sets of polit-if-fides, to fight a war.

On the democratic side, they actually do not want to fight it, they wish to cower in the corner. They think there is no other course than to negotiate our way to victory. There is a time to negotiate and a time to fight. This should not surprise anyone because the people that are ruling the democratic party are the holdovers from the Vietnam era. We are dealing with the same career people in the FBI and the CIA. They are losers who want the nation to keep on losing its standing in the world.

This is supposed to be a memory of the day that things changed. In fact, the best way to honor the people who gave their lives in the attacks is to keep winning the war. We are definitely winning in Iraq and we should not leave until the job is done. The Iraqis have said as much. When we are finished there, we need to concentrate on the business in Afghanistan and Pakistan. In the mountainous area and on the border between those two countries, is where the enemy lies. We need to find ways to get to them and either kill them or get the information that will lead to their leaders being killed or captured.

I am afraid that once we win in Iraq, and move on to Afghanistan and Pakistan, these same nay-sayers will say the some things and try to get us to lose that war also.

That would be great disservice to the people who died in Washington D.C., New York City, and Pennsylvania on that unforgotten day.

Obama's Help On Union Greed
09/12/2008

The labor unions are showing fear and greed. They want to have the power they once had (greed). They also want to take away the rights of their members ability to take a private ballot. That is definitely undemocratic.

We should not be surprised that Barak Obama is for this, he is a far left, socialist after all. Unions, no matter how much they have lost their power, are a part of the American lexicon. They are needed to help keep workers rights in tact. That is why they are needed.

Why should the people in the unions be forced to vote for things that they do not necessarily support? That is what this so called card check bill is all about. It is not only a way for these unions thugs to get around businesses that don't have unions; but, it is also a way for them to force their unionized workers to be in line with how their leaders think and want them to vote.

That card check bill is a thing that Obama is for because he is one of the democrats that has his name on the bill.

If a business does not want to have a union they should not be forced to have one. This is America, after all.

Obama and his buddies in "big unions" are also trying to kill small businesses. Small businesses are the engines of the United States' economy. Unlike the Wal-Mart's Sears', and Costco's, small businesses will not be able to afford fines and other costs that will come with a lengthy fight and negotiation it will take to keep their workers working.

Those are the scary facts. If you are not scared of this, then you should be.

Toughness
09/13/2008

Just how tough is the democratic party?

This is not just me asking this question, it is James Carville.

I do think this is a legitimate question because, it seems the party can not seem to take criticism. Everyone from Barak Obama on down seem to be like little crybabies. Their presidential candidate can not take legitimate criticism on such things, like why he is a friend of Bill Ayers.

I maintain my thought that it (the lack of toughness) stems back to the fact the majority of the leaders of the party are from the time when they were young adulthood protesting the Vietnam War. They are peace nicks. They believe that there is NO, absolutely, NO situation in which war is necessary. This includes if and when we are attacked.

They are so befuddled that they do not know how to handle Sarah Palin.

Carville is correct to fear a loss in the next election. The fact of the matter is that if they lose as big as I think they might, it could hurt them for a generation or more.

Survival Of The Greenest
09/15/2008

The democrats tend to believe the republicans accept more money from special interest groups. That is just not true.

Take Don Cazayoux.

Over the election season, he has kept his campaign afloat with a majority of money ($95,000) coming from these same interest gorups. The majority of these groups are from outside of his district. In fact, they are almost exclusively Washington D.C. groups.

I am not saying it is crooked to accept money from these groups but it is unethical.

This is another reason I, in good conscience, can not bring myself to vote for him.

Perfect Palin
09/16/2008

In a lot of people's estimation, Sarah Palin is the perfect pick for the office of the Vice President.

Even though she is a politician, she comes across as a "regular person." I use this term in the same manner that Malcolm-Jamal Warner as Theodore Huxtable did in the Cosby Show. He was arguing with his dad about his grades when he said that he wanted to be a regular person instead of a doctor, like his father; or a lawyer, like his mother. Mrs. Palin gives off the vibration that she is one of us. This means it appears she is blue collar rather than white collar.

I like this lady because she is living what most American believe in. She has a family. She believes in gun ownership. Look, I don't own a gun, but I believe that one should have a right to. Non-abortion, low taxes, small government, and other such issues are some of the real issues that are important to Americans in the, so-called, fly-over part of the country.

Even tough her family is well of, she is not one of the uber-rich. She and her husband have worked hard for their money. They have payed their taxes.

All in all, she is closer to being one of us than anyone else in this election. Barak Obama has never held a real job. Joe Biden and John McCain have been in Washington for decades and can be considered career politicians.

Palin may, very well, be the most well liked vice presidential candidate in the history of this great country.

Race Changer
09/17/2008

Sarah Palin is definitely a political race changer.

When the democrats decided to try to move on from the Clintons they took awful risk. On the one hand, I understand the party wants to move on from the Clintons; they do not want the baggage. They also do not want Bill anywhere near the White House. On the other hand, they are losing women and blue collar Americans. These are the people that helped to elect Reagan, Bush and Bush. They are what is commonly known as the Reagan democrats.

In a little over two months, the polls have turned around. This far from the election the polls do not matter. As we get closer to the election, the polls take on a different meaning. People, now, are just starting to pay attention to candidates and politics. They gathering information to make their decision on who they will vote for.

Mrs. Palin is a strong conservative woman. We know where she stands and she is not going to change her mind on the issues.

The democrats are deathly afraid of her. They know what she stands for with the young women. She proves that a woman can have it all. She can have a family and a career and is willing to work hard at it. She is willing to have a husband and family and make the serious choices it takes to keep her core beliefs intact.

This woman is a great American story. The democrats are worried they will not be able to darken that story. This means they will not be able to find the dirt it will take to soil her. They think she is too clean. They think just because they have a lot of skeletons in the collective closets, she too has them. It does not work that way. Not everyone has things in their past that would soil their future. That is just too cynical of a world view for me. When voting, a good person should consider a good person.

The democrats are looking as hard as they can for dirt. Sometimes the harder they look, the less they find.

Democrat Fears.
09/18/2008

The democrats are getting paranoid. At one time the general consensus was, even if Barak Obama was not to win, it would be a huge year for the democrats. They expected to take a greater amount of seats in the congress and a greater amount of seats in state legislatures and governorships.

They now fear because of the energy issue and the Obama ticket, their potential big win might not happen. It seems they are losing their confidence. They are definitely having buyers remorse. They have started to think they have picked the wrong nominee.

I tend to agree with them. This man is an empty suit. I would say he is a far-left person, but they all are. Many are beginning to see that he is unqualified. Some democrats are starting to think they should have given the nomination to Obama's vice-presidential nominee, Joe Biden. To that extent, they probably should have chosen Hillary Clinton.

Back to the issue at hand, the so-called huge win for the democrats. It is a scary thought that the democrats will have a greater majority in the house and the senate. It would give them a veto-proof majority. That scares me because this would give them the confidence to pass legislature to raise taxes to great heights.

I will say this, we really can not afford for the democrats to expand their majorities.

Old/New Rules
09/19/2008

The FBI is adopting new rules. Actually, these "new" rules are pretty darn close to those of J. Edgar Hoover in the 1970's.

One good thing is the "wall" that was put up by Jamie Gurellic to stop federal law enforcement and espionage organizations from sharing information has been taken down. That, so-called, rule needed to go and it went.

On these rules changes, it will make it easier for the FBI to prosecute the war on terror.

Sure, it may bring back issuses the civil liberties groups, like the ACLU, don't like; but, to be honest, these are greatly needed. The ACLU is afraid racial profiling will be the order of the day. I say that this is greatly needed. Sure, not all terrorists are Muslims (Bill Ayers), but it seems a great number are. I am not saying all Muslims are bad people. There are some who want nothing to do with the people who are soiling their religion.

The war on terror will be a multi generational war and we need to give the people who protect us the tools they need to prosecute it expeditiously. If we don't, our chances to be attacked will increase.

Step Up And Take The Blame (The Buck Stops Here)
09/20/2008

There were some problems during both hurricanes this year. When evacuees got to some of the shelters, some were not fully prepared. Some of the shelters did not have showers for the evacuees to wash the dirt, grime, and stress off of them.

There were other problems. There were organizational problems with some of the ways benefits were doled out. A good example of this is the emergency food stamp program. When the people were told where to go to get them, they went and found there were long lines and confusion.

When the head of the Department of Social Services, Ann Silverberg Williamson, realized this, she took the blame. That is such a refreshing thing, a government worker admitting to inefficiency. You know, they do work for the people.

Most politicians, when they make mistakes, do not have the guts to take the blame. They are cowards in this respect. This is a definite way to fight the network. Williamson's job is to make sure government programs operate smoothly.

This is another sign there is a new day dawning here in Louisiana. We have been under the dark cloud of the network for so long that we have forgotten what good governance looks like. By no means, am I saying that a year, two, four, or eight will completely change things; but, I do think it is a good start. In all jobs like this it will take the work of several years of straightforward and upright leaders to get this job done.

Why The Fear Of The Truth
09/22/2008

Why is Barak Obama afraid to let people speak? In his home district/state, he has asserted some power in keeping people who have written books criticizing him, off of the radio.

This should not be surprising. He is a democrat and they, in general, are for the fairness doctrine. They do not like to be called on their stupidity.

What is the fairness doctrine? This is a doctrine that states that for every conservative a radio station puts on the air, there must also be a liberal on the station. More insidious is the fact, that stations will be forced to hire liberals on the boards of directors. The way to get around that is to have a rule that states that for every liberal forced to be hired a consevative must be hired.

Back to the issue of why he responding to the people with books that have negative information against him. This is an outgrowth of the fact Sarah Palin has stolen his mojo.

It's Never Good To Be A Rhino
09/23/2008

Rhinos are republicans in name only. That is the worst kind of republican. It seems like they always end up sitting on the fence on every major issue. That is not good.

Arnold Schwartzenegger, for the last five years, has been acting like a rhino republican. It now appears he is itching for a fight over the California state budget. It has been getting bigger and bigger and has become too bloated. Now, it appears both parties in the California legislature want it to get even bigger, but Schartzenegger is about to make a stand. Much like what has happened here in Louisiana, the California legislature is blustering about a veto override session.

Even though California is considered to be the land of fruits, nuts, and flakes, does not mean the people can not rise up and, like here in Louisiana, say enough. The budget the lawmakers in California want to pass will be a bad thing, not only for their state but for the United States as well.

This is exactly why I am happy we Louisianans have elected a true conservative in Bobby Jindal. Not only is he a true conservative, but he is, also, a person that will call a spade a spade. He did this with the problems that exist with the situation of handing out food stamps after the storm.

Back to the subject at hand, California. We all know that state's situation is dire. The fact of the matter is if it does not get fixed it could seriously hurt the country.

For Some, The Dirtier The Better
09/24/2008

Elections can get very dirty, especially, if one side fears the lead is slipping away.

The democrats are showing the fear. This was supposed to be a year in which they were favored to take the presidency, congress, several governorships, and state legislatures. The polls indicate this it not the case. The polls, with respect to generic ballots, say the republican candidates for the congress seats are even with their democrat opponents. If this were any other year, the democrats should be far ahead.

The democrats at all levels are getting down and dirty, and it will get even worse as it gets closer to election day. I am not sure John McCain's running mate, Sarah Palin, can withstand a dirty campaign.

Groups like the National Organization of Women (NOW) and the abortion group, NARAL, are against Palin because of her core beliefs. She has expressed that she is a new feminist. She, and women like her, are pulling off this feat. They have a family and a career. They are yearning for a career to serve the people. That is the new generation of feminism. The previous generation of feminists do not agree and see women making only one choice. They want it to be, either, homemaker or career woman.

This election will be historic because the democrats thought this was supposed to be their year.

It appears the dirt is flying and the American people are quickly tiring of it. If the democrats don't watch themselves, they will hurt the party for the next generation.

Chavez's Machismo
09/25/2008

Hugo Chavez, one of America's top enemies is at it again. He is trying to puff himself up into something more than what he is. He wants to become a world power. This man is nothing more than a "two-bit" communist dictator.

He is starting to make deals with America's enemies. The first thing that he has done is to make a deal with China to purchase some military (jets) hardware. These planes are to be used to train an air force he plans to start up. Chavez, also, wants a navy. He is having the Chinese construct a tanker with the express idea of having a shipyard built. Is it no doubt what will come next? Not in my mind. He wants carriers, as to carry planes, that are probably being built, as we talk.

Why have we not invoked Manifest Destiny or Monroe Doctrine. To all the people that are not history buffs, the Monroe Doctrine is a policy that was dreamed up by President James Monroe. Here is what it stated:

European powers were no longer to colonize or interfere with the affairs of the newly independent states of the Americas. The United States planned to stay neutral in wars between European powers and their colonies.

In an addendum to the policy, President Theodore Roosevelt stated the following:

Extension of the Monroe Doctrine asserted the right of the United States to intervene to stabilize the economic affairs of small nations in the Caribbean and Central America if they were unable to pay their international debts.

I think that the enemies of the United States, of this time are lining up to test, whether or not, we are willing to dust this off and to enforce it. Whomever the next president will be will have to make that decision.

Back to the matter at hand. Chavez has been a thorn in America's side for a long, long time. There will come a time at which we will have to deal with him. I think the time is rapidly coming to the forefront.

New Center Needed
09/28/2008

At times throughout the history of measuring hurricanes, there have been predictions and mistakes made by those tracking them. Measuring hurricanes and the damages wrought by storms have been an inexact science.

Storm surge has always played a part in the damages of the cities closest to the coast. A storm surge center has, in my opinion, been need. When you live as close to the coast as the people it the states of Florida, Alabama, Mississippi, Louisiana, and Texas, the people may not understand politicians, predictions, and other things, but what they know, is that hurricanes can damage property in many ways.

Hurricanes Katrina, Rita, Gustav, and Ike damaged huge amounts of property and an unusual number of people. Storm surges did most of that damage.

Because of Katrina and Rita, a United States geologist, Ben McGee, started a storm surge center, operating from his home. Being an expert in his chosen field of geology, he has invented a new measurement of hurricane damage. Mr. McGee has proven this type of information is needed. We may very well see these storm surge centers crop up in the other gulf coast states. The storm surge damages of New Orleans during Hurricane Katrina was of a different type. It can be blamed on the government, especially the Corps of Engineers.

Palin Is Correct
09/29/2008

On September 22, Sarah Palin was scheduled to speak at a political rally in New. York. Because of objections by the Israeli faction protest against Iran, this rally was cancelled. Hillary Clinton was invited but she refused to appear with Palin I understand why Hillary did not want to appear with Governor Palin. Governor Palin is a younger, more atteractive woman and she is diametrically opposed to Hillary's political views.

I digress.

In terms of the speech Palin would have given, she was right on the mark with her comments.

Here are the Comments:

"I am honored to be with you and with leaders from across this great country — leaders from different faiths and political parties united in a single voice of outrage."

"Tomorrow, Mahmoud Ahmadinejad will come to New York — to the heart of what he calls the Great Satan — and speak freely in this, a country whose demise he has called for."

"Ahmadinejad may choose his words carefully, but underneath all of the rhetoric is an agenda that threatens all who seek a safer and freer world."

"We gather here today to highlight the Iranian dictator's intentions and to call for action to thwart him."

"He must be stopped."

"The world must awake to the threat this man poses to all of us. Ahmadinejad denies that the Holocaust ever took place. He dreams of being an agent in a 'Final Solution' — the elimination of the Jewish people. He has called Israel a 'stinking corpse' that is 'on its way to annihilation'. Such talk cannot be dismissed as the ravings of a madman — not when Iran just this summer tested long-range Shahab-3 missiles capable of striking Tel Aviv, not when the Iranian nuclear program is nearing completion, and not when Iran sponsors terrorists that threaten and kill innocent people around the world."

"The Iranian government wants nuclear weapons. The International Atomic Energy Agency reports that Iran is running at least 3,800 centrifuges and that its uranium enrichment capacity is rapidly improving." "According to news reports, U.S. intelligence agencies believe the Iranians may have enough nuclear material to produce a bomb within a year."

"The world has condemned these activities." The United Nations Security Council has demanded that Iran suspend its illegal nuclear enrichment activities. It has levied three rounds of sanctions."

"How has Ahmadinejad responded? With the declaration that the 'Iranian nation would not retreat one iota' from its nuclear program. So, what should we do about this growing threat? First, we must succeed in Iraq."

"If we fail there, it will jeopardize the democracy the Iraqis have worked so hard to build, and empower the extremists in neighboring Iran. Iran has armed and trained terrorists who have killed our soldiers in Iraq, and it is Iran that would benefit from an American defeat in Iraq."

"If we retreat without leaving a stable Iraq, Iran's nuclear ambitions will be bolstered. If Iran acquires nuclear weapons — they could share them tomorrow with the terrorists they finance, arm, and train today."

"Iranian nuclear weapons would set off a dangerous regional nuclear arms race that would make all of us less safe."

"But Iran is not only a regional threat; it threatens the entire world. It is the no. 1 state sponsor of terrorism. It sponsors the world's most vicious terrorist groups, Hamas and Hezbollah. Together, Iran and its terrorists are responsible for the deaths of Americans in Lebanon in the 1980s, in Saudi Arabia in the 1990s, and in Iraq today."

"They have murdered Iraqis, Lebanese, Palestinians, and other Muslims who have resisted Iran's desire to dominate the region." " They have persecuted countless people simply because they are Jewish."

"Iran is responsible for attacks not only on Israelis, but on Jews living as far away as Argentina."

" Anti-Semitism and Holocaust denial are part of Iran's official ideology and murder is part of its official policy. Not even Iranian citizens are safe from their government's threat to those who want to live, work, and worship in peace."

" Politically-motivated abductions, torture, death by stoning, flogging, and amputations are just some of its state-sanctioned punishments."

"It is said that the measure of a country is the treatment of its most vulnerable citizens."

"By that standard, the Iranian government is both oppressive and barbaric."

" Under Ahmadinejad's rule, Iranian women are some of the most vulnerable citizens."

"If an Iranian woman shows too much hair in public, she risks being beaten or killed."

"If she walks down a public street in clothing that violates the state dress code, she could be arrested."

"But in the face of this harsh regime, the Iranian women have shown courage."

" Despite threats to their lives and their families, Iranian women have sought better treatment through the 'One Million Signatures Campaign Demanding Changes to Discriminatory Laws'."

"The authorities have reacted with predictable barbarism. Last year, women's rights activist Delaram Ali was sentenced to 20 lashes and 10 months in prison for committing the crime of 'propaganda against the system'."

"After international protests, the judiciary reduced her sentence to 'only' 10 lashes and 36 months in prison and then temporarily suspended her sentence. She still faces the threat of imprisonment."

"Earlier this year, Senator Hillary Clinton said that 'Iran is seeking nuclear weapons, and the Iranian Revolutionary Guard Corps is in the forefront of that effort'. Senator Clinton argued that part of our response must include stronger sanctions, including the designation of the IRGC as a terrorist organization. John McCain and I could not agree more."

"Senator Clinton understands the nature of this threat and what we must do to confront it." This is an issue that should unite all Americans. Iran should not be allowed to acquire nuclear weapons. Period. And in a single voice, we must be loud enough for the whole world to hear: Stop Iran! Only by working together, across national, religious, and political differences, can we alter this regime's dangerous behavior."

"Iran has many vulnerabilities, including a regime weakened by sanctions and a population eager to embrace opportunities with the West." We must increase economic pressure to change Iran's behavior."

"Tomorrow, Ahmadinejad will come to New York." On our soil, he will exercise the right of freedom of speech — a right he denies his own people." He will share his hateful agenda with the world. "Our task is to focus the world on what can be done to stop him."

"We must rally the world to press for truly tough sanctions at the U.N. or with our allies if Iran's allies continue to block action in the U.N. We must start with restrictions on Iran's refined petroleum imports."

"We must reduce our dependency on foreign oil to weaken Iran's economic influence."

"We must target the regime's assets abroad; bank accounts, investments, and trading partners."

"President Ahmadinejad should be held accountable for inciting genocide, a crime under international law."

"We must sanction Iran's Central Bank and the Revolutionary Guard Corps — which no one should doubt is a terrorist organization."

"Together, we can stop Iran's nuclear program. Senator McCain has made a solemn commitment that I strongly endorse: Never again will we risk another Holocaust."

"And this is not a wish, a request, or a plea to Israel's enemies. This is a promise that the United States and Israel will honor, against any enemy who cares to test us." It is John McCain's promise and it is my promise."

"Thank you."

She is correct about the danger Ahmadinejad poses and the negative pressures that he has put on his own people.

The lack of freedom for that nation's women is appalling. Where is the National Organization for Women and other such groups. Whatever freedoms they once had are gone. They are routinely punished for doing things that the women in this country take for granted. Yet they keep doing them. That is a true definition of bravery and standing up for what you believe in.

Ahmadinejad and his supportors keep thumbing their noses at the rest of the world. We keep telling them not to enrich uranium but they keep disobeying. They don't seem to be affected by the sanctions, even though the sanctions are severe ones. It is looking more and more like the rest of the world will have to use the military option to discipline Iran.

Sarah Palin is correct in her speech and the phraseology that she used.